Working Girl
My 20 Years In The Business

by
Eliana

Published in March 2011 by emp3books,
Kiln Workshops, Pilcot Road, Crookham Village,
Fleet, Hampshire, GU51 5RY, England

©**Eliana**

The author asserts the moral right to be identified as the author of this
work

ISBN: 978-1-907140-35-8

Copyright registered with Copyright Protection Service
3 February 2011

**emp3
books**

www.emp3books.com

DEDICATION

This book is dedicated to my mother who has supported me loyally and lovingly throughout my life, to my children who I adore, to my partner and to all the working girls who have been part of my life.

Eliana

26 February 2011

CONTENTS

vi

Chapter1
INTRODUCTION

It's 4.00 in the afternoon. I'm sitting in a well-worn armchair in the girls' room, waiting, hoping, longing for the sauna's doorbell to chime. The day has been too quiet for comfort and so far I have only done one client. He was one of my regulars. All he wants is a 10 minute massage followed by hand-relief. That's only £40 so far today and I've got a lot of bills coming in at the end of the month.

I'm 5'9", slim with nice breasts. I'm wearing a red bra and panties with black fish-net hold-ups and red 5" stilettos. On top is a white overall to give the effect of being a nurse but with enough buttons undone for clients to get excited by a glimpse of what is on offer. My legs are beautiful and my body is permanently light brown as I am mixed race. My eyes are brown and my dark hair is down to below my shoulders. I'm in my early 40s and I'm aware that even when I'm out in public and dressed quite ordinarily I still attract attention. I like to be looked at – most girls do - because I want the reassurance that I can go on being a working girl for a bit longer if I have to.

At last the doorbell rings. I switch the TV set to the CCTV camera in the foyer. Jackie, the girl I am working with today, and I take a peek. We don't recognize the man so he may be new, though also he may have come on a day when other girls were working. I feel that buzz of expectancy even after 20 years in the business. Will he be a big spender or will he haggle about a price and then simply walk away? Both Jackie and I badly need the cash. Because Jackie did the last customer it should be my turn. We both go to the foyer's door and look through the spy-hole. The guy looks OK. We unlock the door and he steps back a pace.

"Hello, darling" we say in our friendliest way. "Been here before?" He shakes his head. New customer. Dressed tidily. Could be worth £70 upwards. Could become a regular.

"What are you looking for, darling?" asks Jackie. He pauses and seems nervous? Oh no, is he going to duck out?

"How many girls are there today?"

1

"Just the two of us."

He is looking us over. Jackie's tits are bigger than mine but my legs are longer. I wonder if he's a tits man or a legs man.

He pauses again and gives a nervous smile.

"Will you do a two-girl?"

We both smile back at him. "Course we will, darling. You'll have fun. It's £100".

He looks furtive. "I've only got £70". We've heard that one plenty of times.

"Sorry, darling, that's not enough. But as you haven't been before we'll do it for £90. Just this time. Let's talk about what you like inside. He nods and crosses the threshold. We lock the door again. We are in the passage that leads to the treatment rooms.

"Tell us what you are looking for". He lists a few things.

"That's OK, darling, but with a condom."

We take him into a room.

"Will you pay now please, darling?" He puts notes in my hands. I count them. Yes, there's £90.

"Like to take a shower first?" He shakes his head. "Cup of tea?"

"Milk and one sugar, please". Jackie goes out to make it.

I hear the telephone in the girls' room. "I'll be back in a minute. Make yourself comfortable". I hurry out because I can't miss the call while Jackie's in the kitchen.

Five minutes later we are both back in the room and I close the door behind us. He's lying on the massage table, face upward, legs spread wide, naked. Jackie and I look at his cock to see what we will be working with. It's

2

average size and it's half hard already. We unbutton our nurses' overalls and unhook our bras. He watches us intently. Jackie and I look at each other and smile. We like working together. He'll be done in under half an hour.

The day is looking up.

Chapter 2
EARLY DAYS

I'm an East-Ender by birth and proud of it. I talk Cockney and have never tried to change. It's the way I am. It's how I talk to friends, my partner, my kids and, of course, clients.

My mother is white and my father was West African. Not that I ever really knew him. He had dropped out of my mum's life by the time I was born. I'm not too sure whether I came about as a result of a real relationship or just a flirtation. It is the kind of thing that is too sensitive to ask your mum and anyway what matters much more is how she treated me and brought me up.

I'm a tough cookie and my survival skills are down to my kind loyal mother who gave me a loving childhood that built the foundations which have enabled me to survive to this day. Actually I think my mum cared for my dad but he lied to her. He told her he was single but one day his wife found out, came along to my nan's house and spilled the beans. That must have been an awful experience for my mum, not least because I was well on the way.

This was in the swinging 'sixties when traditional family patterns were breaking down fast. The Pill, which is taken for granted these days, had changed everyone's attitude to sex. In essence, women used to have to be the careful ones. The Pill changed all that and people took risks assuming that the girl would not get pregnant. I was a baby from that era.

Because of the Pill women were expected to be up for sex whenever they wanted it. Because men always want sex, girls became the decision-makers whereas in the past they often said 'no'. They may have wanted sex but they were afraid of the consequences of pregnancies. Illegitimate children, as they were called, were still looked on as something rather shameful when I was born.

It was no longer up to the man to use a condom because women were expected to be on the Pill. In those days Aids hadn't been discovered and other forms of sexually transmitted disease were hardly known and still less talked about. Syphilis and gonorrhoea were in the history books. Nobody thought about Chlamydia and genital warts.

My mum was part of that era. It might be OK to have sex with a boyfriend but it wasn't OK to produce kids without a husband. And it was even worse to produce a mixed race baby without a dad. Of course things have changed fundamentally since then and there are plenty of relationships, many of them long term, where a girl has kids without being married and sometimes by different dads. I am from one of those families and that's the way my life has worked out too.

My grandparents on my mother's side had traditional, rather Victorian family values. My mother was married and had a son who is seven years older than me. His dad was white and my brother was brought up as part of a conventional family. All hell was let loose when my mum told her parents that she was pregnant again and that this time the dad was West African. It seems hard to imagine it now but she came back from work one day and they told her she had to find somewhere else to live. They were the kind of people who minded about what the neighbours would say.

So when my mum was about four months pregnant with me she found herself having to make arrangements not just for somewhere to live with her new baby but also for a carer. She had an office job which she had to break off for my birth but which she needed to get back to so that she could pay the rent and the carer as well as for nappies and baby-clothes. You might say that I wasn't born with a silver spoon in my mouth.

My elder half-brother continued to live with my grandparents. They loved him and gave him a good education at fee-paying schools. For many years I didn't see anything of him but later, when my grandparents' attitudes towards me had softened, we met quite a lot and became close. He is white, well-spoken and his good education has enabled him to get good jobs.

My dad

I got to see more of my mum's family when I started to become good at gymnastics. This was when I went to my first school. The rest of my family were very Victorian in outlook and looked on my mum as the black sheep of the family but when they realised that I was a talented gymnast they became much warmer to me and my mum.

6

We have a very wealthy uncle and auntie who idolised my brother and gave him all sorts of treats and privileges which never came my way. They took him on holidays and even on a trip in the Queen Elizabeth II but I was always left at home with my mum. When we did start meeting, like all elder brothers he used to tease me a lot as his kid-sister and at times I hated him for it.

His life hasn't turned out perfectly. He has been divorced and had other difficulties so, in a funny sort of way, it is me he now turns to when he wants a shoulder to cry on even though he remains the white sheep of the family and I'm the black one. By most standards, he has been the success story and I have been the opposite.

My mother was given a one-bedroom flat in a high-rise block in the East End. At the time my brother was living with my nan, but when he was a teenager he came back to live with my mum and me in the high-rise. He didn't really bully me and because of the age difference between us and because I never had a dad, I looked up to him as a father figure.

Actually I did get to meet my dad just a handful of times but that doesn't make for a proper relationship. The first time I met him I was at my nan's. I used to spend a lot of time with her and she idolised me. One day I was in her garden and doing my gymnastics which I was always doing because it was the main thing in my life. I heard her calling me and I looked back at the window and I could see a tall dark fellow by the window. Without being told I instantly knew it was my dad. I was eight at the time and it was my mum's wish that I would never see him.

I remember cart-wheeling back to the end of the garden. My nan came out and he stood there by the rose-arch. She said: "Come here. I want you to meet someone". I walked back down and she said: "This is your dad". I smiled and he commented on what a pretty girl I was. My nan told him I was a talented athlete. I didn't know what to say to him because I was a shy girl. I just remember smiling and walking away and carrying on with my gymnastics in the garden. That was my first meeting with my dad.

When I got home I told my mum and she was absolutely livid. Furious, furious, furious. My mum and my nan hadn't got on for many years but even so my nan used to visit us because she idolised me. When she came the atmosphere in the house was frosty. My nan would be left sitting in the

7

lounge with me and I used to dance for her. She would sit there clapping her hands and I was always the showgirl. My mum would make herself busy round the house and there were many occasions when no words were exchanged between mother and daughter. On various occasions my nan would say "Your mum doesn't like me at all". I picked up very early as a child that my mum hated her mum coming to visit, and when my nan had introduced me to my dad that made matters worse.

On a few occasions after that I met him again at my nan's house but it was literally nothing more than a hello. I was a shy girl and on his part I think wanting to see me was just curiosity. Then I didn't see him for many years until I was in my twenties. When I started driving I decided to drive to the East end of London to visit him because I knew where he lived. I called his wife Auntie Cynthia. She was black, short and stout and rather ugly. She used to sit in her chair and stare at me, picking her chin. Just stare, stare, stare at me. She had had my dad's children and she used to comment how beautiful I was. I was the mixed race kid. I felt when she looked at me she didn't like me.

I never stayed long at my dad's because I didn't know what to say to him. I was offered food and things but it was just a game. It had been too long. I never bonded with him. I used to tell my mum when I was going to see him. By then she was OK about it because she knew I wasn't going to strike up any relationship or go and live with him.

Many years after that — I'd had a child of my own by then — something came strongly into my head. I felt the need to go to see him. One evening I drove there and parked opposite his house. I could tell by the curtains they were still living there. I knocked on the door and there was no answer but there was a light from the upstairs bedroom. I looked through the letterbox and I knew my dad wasn't there. He used to wear a trilby hat and it always used to hang over the banister post. The hat wasn't there.

Auntie Cynthia shouted out from the stairs: "Is that you, Eliana?" And I shouted back through the door: "Yes, it's me". She came down the stairs very slowly and I knew instantly she was going to tell me that my dad was gone. Dead.

She opened the door and said "Robbie's not here. You're too late. He died two months ago."

She brought me in and I stayed for about an hour. She showed me photos of the funeral and some earlier ones of him. When he was younger he was the absolute image of Mohammed Ali. He had died of brain cancer and had had a wonderful send-off. She asked me if there was anything of his that I wanted. I asked for his hat and a photograph. She offered me his car and a few other things. She was going to sell the house and go back to America where her children were. I was meant to go back a week later to sort things out, but I never went back. So I never took his car, I never took anything, I just never went back.

Despite not having a dad I had a happy childhood. Quite early on my mum got a better flat in another part of East London and I went to primary school there. It was then I discovered that I was very talented at athletic things such as running and gymnastics in particular. I am quite a tall girl now, 5' 9" to be exact, but at primary school when I was eight or nine I was about the same height as the other kids. I had a wonderful teacher and he put together a team of six girls to represent the school and the borough at gymnastics. I passed various exams and soon became the team leader. I was daring and I had plenty of stamina and determination. I won medals and prizes and for three years in a row I was the top gymnast and the fastest runner in my borough.

My coach had great faith in me and felt that I could go much further. He had connections with a club in south-east London where a lot of British gymnasts trained under a former British Olympic gymnast. She spotted my potential and picked me out from my school team as the one she wanted to train personally. My head of year at school was very supportive and allowed me out of school, sometimes a bit early, to go to regular training sessions. She really adored me and knew that I was a credit to the school. So four or five times a week my mum would collect me from school and I would go to the Ladywell gym in south-east London for intense training sessions of two or three hours. Here I found myself training alongside several gymnasts who went on to represent Great Britain.

Then, when I was eleven I had an accident. I was practising on the beam, which was one of my favourites and learning to do a summersault. This was just becoming a new movement on the beam though it became routine ten years or so later. I misjudged my landing and fell badly, fracturing both my ankles. They rushed me to Lewisham hospital and initially I was paralysed from my ankles to above my waist. When I was sent home it took me a long time to recover. During this time I felt badly jarred and I lost interest in gymnastics but after a bit I decided I wanted to try again. This was partly in gratitude to my mum who was so loyal to me as a single mum well before single mums became commonplace, and also because my trainer at school had spent so much time on me. So after about nine months I got back to school and back to gymnastics training.

Six months later I had the same accident and that was it. My ankles healed though they were always weak. But gymnastics were finished for me at the age of twelve. I had given it everything I could for five years and now the dream was over. This was the first time in my life that I came to experience depression.

The combination of having missed a lot of schooling, firstly for training and then from injuries, meant that I only took three GCSEs. I look back on childhood and my time at school as happy but when I left school I had no idea what I wanted to do. On my final report the headteacher wrote "this girl will go cart-wheeling through life".

Uncle Nick

In the early '70s when I was seven, a family member I'd never heard of before came to stay. I later learned he was the adopted son of my grandma's half sister. He was a short man with a mop of red hair and face as red to match. I was told to call him Uncle Nick.

I don't think my mum was too keen on him. She used to say he was sly and irritating. He had a twitch and a stammer and it would take him ages to get his words out. Nevertheless my mum was a kind woman and took him in as his marriage had broken down and he needed somewhere to stay for a short while. He was handy for my mum at times as he could look after me while she went out. Not that she went out much as she was a very good single parent and very rarely went anywhere without me.

One of her favourite outings was visiting her old school chum, Mary, who had been evacuated during the war. I loved Auntie Mary as she made an awful fuss of me because she was childless. My mum would stay quite late and I hated the journey home, especially when we got to Woolwich Arsenal as we would have to walk that horrible tunnel a mile long and then take another bus home. So on some occasions it would work out that Uncle

10

Nick would look after me and my mum would go and visit, relax and talk about old times without me whingeing when it was time to go home.

As I was always the exhibitionist Uncle Nick became my audience and I would sing and dance in front of him as I always did for grandma. One day my mum said "Goodbye, Lou-Lou." That was my nickname. "Be a good girl" and off she went to visit Auntie Mary. I was dancing and prancing around my mum's living room as usual when Uncle Nick disappeared into the back room.

"Come here, Lou-Lou", he shouted. "I've got something to show you."

I walked in to find Uncle Nick with his trousers at his ankles and this thing sticking out between his legs. I froze but was curious to see what it was.

"Come here" he said and placed my little hand on that thing and started to move my hand back and forth. Within a few minutes some white stuff came out from the end and into my hand. He quickly pulled his trousers up and told me to wash my hands and never to tell anybody as I would be in big trouble. He then gave me two threepenny bits. God, I thought, I can buy a whole lot of sweets. As I loved sweets I didn't think it was too bad.

As I lay in my bed that night I remember thinking I will never tell anyone in the world. Uncle Nick's words were ringing in my ears. "If you tell you will be in serious trouble for being a bad girl". I was so scared I would be sent away, far away, and I would never see my mum or grandma again.

My mum visited Auntie Mary frequently and Uncle Nick's games were just as frequent. He would always give me money — sometimes all the change in his pocket. I used to hide it in the back of my favourite doll called Tiny Tears. I still have her. Although I did what he wanted obligingly it was slowly becoming apparent to me that Uncle Nick was a bad man and would also be in trouble. I came to hate him, hate hate hate him. But I was frightened. I was only small and I felt that I was the one who was very bad.

But I soon got tired of wanking him off and after the dirty deed I would go to my bedroom and cuddle my doll and cry. No more singing and dancing for Uncle Nick. I became tearful and quiet and my grandma noticed it. One day she asked what was wrong. I so wanted to tell her but I couldn't because of what Uncle Nick had said.

11

My mum found my stash of money hidden in my doll and I was accused of stealing money from her and Uncle Nick. Because of my secret and what Uncle Nick had said, there was no other way out but to admit to something I hadn't done. My mother had a belt. She didn't often use it on me and only if I was very naughty. Sometimes she would use a rolled dishcloth to swipe my legs but this time she pulled up my skirt and she gave me a real belting on my bum and my legs. What was worse, Uncle Nick was in the room next door and heard exactly what was going on. In fact he may have watched. When it was over he walked through the room into the kitchen. I'm sure he enjoyed hearing the sound of the belt on me and hearing me cry. He said I was a no-good little thief.

I was sent to my bedroom until the next morning. I cried all day and I made my dolly cry too by pressing her tummy which made tears come out of her eyes. Tiny Tears was my favourite, my only friend.

Strangely enough though, during the next few days my mum seemed to be very nice to me. Then, walking with me in the park she asked me if Uncle Nick had ever touched me. I was stunned and rather than answer, still less tell the truth, I ran off to the swings. I was so frightened I felt sick. "God, she knows…That's why my mum is being nice to me. She is planning to have me sent away".

But mercifully Uncle Nick was soon gone and never seen again. To this day we don't speak of him, so I guess she kind of knew.

I was free, or so I thought. What I didn't know is that what Uncle Nick did to me was to shape and haunt the rest of my life. I had trusted Uncle Nick and I kept the secret close to me for years. He became the first of many men in my life who abused me and let me down.

Sexual awakening

I became sexually aware when about 13. Around that time most of the girls in my year at school were going with boys. My first experience of full sex was with a boy in a graveyard and I remember it feeling very nice. I wasn't quite sure what was supposed to be going on but I liked it. It was the closeness and I wanted to do it again. I was well on with puberty. I had pubic hair and nice breasts. So I went on doing it with other school kids. I quickly discovered that boys, like men, adore having a blowjob. No

12

condoms, of course. One boy I used to go with quite a lot would nick a condom from his dad sometimes for fear of getting me pregnant, in which case the shit would have hit the fan, but he was the exception. Sex was usually in the graveyard or sometimes in their garage, or if their parents were out it would be in their house.

In the early days I never got an orgasm and I only discovered how to do that by playing with myself when I was about 14. That's when I realised what the man is meant to be doing. Hold on a minute. It's not meant to be just a quick fuck, fuck, fuck by the man. There's more to sex than that. In fact I enjoy masturbating and always have. Clients don't give me any physical pleasure even if they are rubbing my clit and even though I'm a clitty girl and still get wonderful orgasms this way. Being a working girl for twenty years hasn't changed that at all.

Chapter 3
MY FIRST CONTACTS WITH
THE GAME

When we moved out of the high-rise block, my mum was given a very pretty maisonette on the outskirts of Essex. We had three large bedrooms and an ample sized garden. We were very happy. Soon we got to work on laying a lawn which was to become the practice area for my gymnastics. Downstairs lived Molly, a large woman of the same age as my mum and the mother of nine children though only three were living with her. I was delighted to find they were of mixed race, being half Indian. She was a no-nonsense woman, a typical East-Ender. Her front door was always open. She liked wheeling and dealing and swore like a docker but her heart was big. She became my second mum and I probably spent more time in her place than I did in mine.

Over the years I got to meet all her other children. Some were from previous marriages and two had been adopted. They were all white apart from the family she had now. When one of her daughters, Jackie, came to stay we struck up a unique relationship. She lived with her dad and had been to boarding school. It was when Molly became very sick that Jackie came to stay so she could look after the three children who were about my age. She would often speak to me in the front bedroom window and we would listen to music. And she would give me alcohol though I was only 13. She was my best friend and I loved her. I so wanted to grow up.

Jackie had wild ways, sleeping with men and staying out late. She soon became pregnant. Molly recovered from cancer and Jackie moved to a house in Forest Gate.

My career as a gymnast was over after the accidents and I was fast becoming a rebellious teenager. I would bunk off school and spend my days with Jackie drinking and getting stoned. Whilst living there Jackie had become friends with a pretty Italian woman called Julia, who was also a wild and heavy drinker. All three of us got on in spite of the age difference and I was soon in on the secret. Julia was on the game. I also learned that Jackie went with her sometimes. I was intrigued and infatuated with them, seeing their lifestyle, always with new clothes and plenty of money. I wanted to be like them. I didn't want to go to school anymore. And I knew from my experience with Uncle Nick that I could wank a man easily, though I never told them about him.

I begged them to take me with them one night. They didn't want to as I was so young and Jackie always felt she had a sense of responsibility towards me. I kept on insisting that I wanted to come too. One day they relented. We got on the Number 25 bus to Earls Court where all the Arabs were. Most evenings we were able to 'turn tricks'. What they wanted was blow-jobs or full sex but I always used a condom.

On the street I would make eye contact with men but I never got into cars. There were plenty of hotels around Earls Court and I would follow them back. On one occasion, it wasn't for the man himself but for his young son. I should say he was about 12 or 13. I gave him a blowjob. In those days street working was a bit cheaper than going to a house. I used to get about £30 - £50 for a trick and I could do four or five men in an evening.

Generally everything was fine and Jackie kept an eye on me but one night there as a fight. A West Indian who was one of Jackie's regulars wanted to go with me instead of her. He tried it on me and Jackie wouldn't let him because she was protective of me. So the two of them had a real fight. Jackie was a large girl who could look after herself and in the end he just went off. That was the only bad experience around that time.

I had no difficulty giving men tricks. Jackie had told me what to expect and what to charge. And if I did only three or four tricks a night I could make £150 easily. It felt good to know I was probably the only 15 year old girl at school who had money. I would buy clothes and perfume and leave them at Jackie's house.

One night I got caught by the police. Jackie, Julia and I were taken to a nearby police station. I was crying so much I couldn't even tell them my name. "Do your parents know you are out "tomming"?" the policewoman asked. Sobbing uncontrollably I shook my head. "Please don't tell my mum". Tomming means looking for men like tom cats. I was so scared. They asked for my address and stupidly I gave it them. They let Jackie and me go but they kept Julia as I guess she was known to them. They never contacted my mum. The next day I vowed I would never do that again. I

16

went back to school and took my GCSEs. I passed in English, maths and history.

My first job on leaving school was in a big fashion retail company in Oxford Street. My sordid past was behind me, or so I thought. The next two years were spent in that company. I enjoyed the job at first but I grew bored of it and the wages didn't give me the lifestyle I craved. My mum suggested I should try nursing. This seemed a good idea so I applied, passed the interview and started training to be a state enrolled nurse at Whipps Cross Hospital, Leytonstone. I loved hospital life. The nurses were fun, especially the Irish. There were loads of parties and I made great friends. I stayed for three years and passed my exams. Looking back, those were the best years of my life.

I also did baby-sitting in the evening for a lady called Marilyn in East Ham. I got on with her straight away. She was attractive with waist-length dark hair. One night she confided in me that she was an escort.

Her life-style immediately tempted me. Fur coats, a lovely house and jewellery. I told her about my previous experience in Earls Court and asked her if she could get me a job. Her best friend ran a high class agency in Kensington. She was reluctant because I was so young, but she set it up for me anyway.

My first job was with an Arab. I was so nervous. In fact there was a group of us along with Marilyn and me. We went to a hotel and split up to go to different rooms. I remember sitting on the side of the bed as I undressed with him watching me. Then when he undressed he only had one arm. It had been amputated and it frightened me. Here was my first proper client and he was like that. He didn't speak almost any English to I just let him get on with it. He wanted straight sex and it seemed to me that he took ages. It was a weird experience and I wanted to cry. Despite this, when he paid me £300 that was the end of my nursing career.

In the early days and for quite some time I used to feel like crying particularly if the client wanted to do things I didn't like. I have never enjoyed anal, but if the client wanted it and was willing to pay enough for it, it would happen. You just get on with it because you want to be paid. Working girls like me have made a choice to go into the business but even so we sometimes feel like victims of circumstances.

17

I made thousands of pounds, opening several different bank accounts and stashing the money. I had to be careful as I was still at home with mum. I was easily led and soon began to drink and do drugs. Many of the working girls did "dabbing" which meant taking sulphate. They also did cocaine which was easily affordable because of the money we were earning. Sulphate in particular makes you chatty and friendly which of course made you very popular with the clients. You could take sulphate by putting it in a little Rizla cigarette paper and swallowing it with a can of Coke. Then when you went home you would still be buzzing and that is when you started drinking, smoking cannabis and taking sleeping pills.

I got sick and depressed and sometimes couldn't be bothered to turn up for jobs. I hated walking into hotels for fear of being stopped. On a few occasions I was stopped and it reminded me of what I was. I really didn't want to be a working girl. I just wanted the money.

My conscience caught up with me so I decided to get clean and free from that world. I was getting used to sulphate and cocaine but I wasn't fully addicted. Even so the come-down was awful. These drugs suppress your appetite and my body ached for days. I didn't have a problem with kicking the drugs because I was so determined. I didn't want to be working, I didn't want to be doing drugs or drinking. I have always believed I was worth a bit more than that. So it was quite easy for me at the time to let go of all of it, to stop, full stop. I took time off. My mum was getting suspicious and I think she really knew but never asked any questions. I went to Spain for a few weeks with some friends and I came back looking beautiful and healthy but skint.

My local gym which I went to regularly was advertising for a gym instructress. I fitted the bill. I was athletic, had a good knowledge of the equipment, was attractive and, as I have been told all my life, my personality is fun and infectious. I got the job.

On my way out feeling happy, I walked along the High Street in Dalston and noticed a sauna with "staff required" on the door. I had just landed my dream job with the gym so there was nothing to lose and I went in. A tall girl in a white overall came to the desk. I asked her about the job. "Have you worked in saunas before?" she asked. "Do you know what happens?" "You are very pretty" she added. She took me to the back and explained. She said I would make a lot of money. "We have around 20-30 clients a

18

day. Would you like me to give you a shift this week and see how you go?" I agreed. I had nothing to lose. I had the job at the gym anyway. I said to myself that I would do that: just one shift. Make some good money for the last time and then get some decent clothes to start my new job with.

"There's a new girl today, darling", the receptionist kept repeating. The phone never stopped and neither did I. There were three of us on a shift, and as I was new everybody wanted to try me. I came home that night on Cloud Nine with £500 and the boss had offered me three shifts a week. I never took my dream job at the gym.

But the nightmare was to unfold for me over the next 20 years. It was about to destroy everything and all those around me. Amidst the glamour, money and material things was the dark, sordid side of being a working girl: the pimps, drugs, beatings. It was a very sad and lonely road I was about to travel.

Chapter 4
LEARNING THE ROPES

Working in saunas

Taking the job in the sauna was the fork in the road that determined my life onwards. The money was way above whatever I could have earned as a nurse or as a trainer in the gym. Once you have got used to having money it is hard to go back to how it was before. The sauna had a large number of clients and this offered guaranteed high earnings.

The routine then was pretty much as now. The client would come in, pay the receptionist the entrance fee and she would bring him through to the lounge area. He would always be kept separate from other clients. Here he would meet the girls. Typically there would be three of us per shift. He would look at us all, choose who he wanted and the girl would take him upstairs. The massage was just an introduction and what was more important was the service that he wanted. She would discuss the fee for this and then they would get on with it.

You might think that it was hurtful to be looked over like prize cattle but in the early days it didn't seem like that. There were plenty of clients so all the girls were busy. But when you get on a bit it does become distasteful. "Do you do this, do you do that and then thank you but I'll have the other girl." After a few years you don't like having them look you over. That's why all working girls like to have their regulars – clients who know what they will get from their particular girl. We always used to say that the clients who spend most time choosing turn out to be the ones who are no good.

Some saunas didn't let the client choose. He just took the first girl who was up. In my first sauna I was lucky. The madam was a clever lady and she chose girls with experience, in their 30s or older. I was much younger so you might have thought they would be jealous and bitchy but they were nice to me. It was a closely run place; the girls had all been there for many years and they all had their own regulars anyway. They liked to get me busy and I was very lucky to work there. Also they would give me tips about certain clients to be careful of who would try things on, for example trying to get away with not wearing a condom.

I stayed in that sauna for about a year. In the sauna world you quickly become acquainted with other girls. It's not unusual to sit in a place for 12 hours with another girl so that if you are on the same wavelength you become friendly very quickly and end up knowing each other's life story in no time. This means that you find that other girls have other shifts in other saunas and flats. Sauna bosses are always on the lookout for girls so you get connections. Sometimes places go quiet so you decide to give another place a try. You end up working a couple of shifts in this one and a couple in that one.

The boss was a well known ex-working girl with many connections. The place was rented from a big East End villain, so there were no problems. Footballers, rock musicians and peers would cross our paths.

Madam X, our boss, was a proper business woman. If a client came in at five to eleven at night we had to stay no matter what or we would lose our jobs. She was a no-nonsense woman, hard as nails, but I respected her, admired her in fact. She liked me instantly when I was first introduced to her by a lovely girl who had worked with her years before and had started working for her when she set up her own place. These were the old school of sauna girls and they were the best.

A year or so passed and I became tired of four shifts a week with eleven-hour days or more. When we left the sauna we sometimes went on to party with the clients who were always heavily drunk or stoned. They may have been famous or infamous but at 5.00 a.m in the morning reality hits hard and you just wanted to go home.

These parties varied with the boss I was working for. Sometimes the boss would ask certain girls to go and you would get paid a lump sum of a few hundred quid. But the clients were always on the gear, on the coke. It was about them enjoying themselves. They just wanted good-time girls with them. It was more about getting out of your head than the sexual side of things. The way you would look at it was as a fun night out. Drugs were there, drink was there. It wasn't going to cost you anything. You might have to get it off with a few of their mates in some place they had hired, but a lot of the time, because they were coked up, nothing really came of it. Just a lot of fun. We'd all be pissed and get on with the party. Sometimes we would have sexual fun with them. We'd be on cocaine too and the drug makes you lose all your inhibitions so you could be prancing around with nothing on.

Because I was still very fresh and with a superb figure I was popular with clients so I could have stayed where I was for a long time but I was to change saunas. Working with one or two girls on a shift and then different girls on the next shift you get acquainted with other girls very easily. You have a drink and spell out your life story to each other in a day. Quickly you find out how girls work in different saunas and flats. Word of mouth was the way girls moved around. "Why don't you try the place I'm at? You'd do well there. I'm working there tomorrow and I'll have a word."

Because our community of working girls is enclosed as far as the outside world is concerned, girls were helpful in finding openings for each other. Those were the days of plenty of money and plenty of clients. Girls weren't really competing for work. There was enough for all of us. It was all very short term. Another day, another dollar. Things aren't like that now as I'll explain later.

I left Madam X's sauna after a year or so but I took with me knowledge and wisdom. I had walked into the place as green as grass. I left a proper working girl. I had learned that the sauna world is a world of its own. There are special codes and lines you don't cross.

The first big rule is not to get involved with clients on a personal level. Don't tell them where you live or anything about you or your kids. If you have a half hour chatting session in my experience it is half an hour of lies. It's not your real name, you don't live where you've just said you live and you've got three kids, not one kid. You learn very quickly not to trust anyone. After 20 years in the business I have learned not to trust anyone, not anyone. Number One lesson: trust no-one.

Different saunas had different rules. Some were more relaxed. Some didn't like you taking your mobile phone into the room; some didn't like you working in other places; some didn't like you working with friends. If they thought you were too friendly they would split you up because they thought you might be cooking the books. Some would even send "clients" in to see if you were playing the game properly like charging the right sort of money. It might be a Harry Flash type of guy sent to try and entice you: "Would you

23

like to go out with me?" kind of thing. You could fall for that and then find out it was a good friend of the boss and you would be out of a job. If you know that bosses will send men in you don't know, you have to play by the rules.

The other big rule I discovered was a personal one. I found that working girls need a big heart. We are all there for one thing: to earn the money, but life in the business isn't easy and all of us find it gets us down sometimes. Actually that is true for most jobs in the outside world but it is more acute, more painful for a working girl. That is why for many of us a sense of humour and laughter are our defence mechanisms.

For example, in all the saunas where we worked they played music quite loud so that individual clients would not hear what was happening in the room next door. We still do this in my sauna. In some saunas there were loudspeakers in each room. One of the songs which kept on coming up in the tapes that were played was Private Dancer sung by Tina Turner. This song is all about what a private dancer does for clients and so was very near to the bone as far as we were concerned. So as soon as the song began we would start a new conversation with the client so as to distract him. The words of the song are very sharp and made us working girls squirm as did any song that referred to what we were doing.

When I left Madam X's sauna I went to meet a woman who had just opened a sauna on her own. This was in the '80s when everyone had money and people were branching out. Poppy had been a working girl for 15 years more than me so she was ready to do her own thing and be in control of her own life. It's a big step up from just working.

Poppy's sauna was like a breath of fresh air. Instead of the old table lamps and frilly curtains it had a clean clinical look that worked. The walls were magnolia, the reception desk was smart and it had a Jacuzzi. To begin with it was slow like all new places. You had to be patient and build up your clientele. The shift money we had to pay was more but you charged the clients more. If you stuck it out and were good at your job it nearly always paid off. The hours were longer. A typical shift was eleven or twelve hours which made for a fucking long day at times. This sauna was situated on a main road just on the London-Essex border so it got a lot of attention and all sorts of clients from your average working man to influential people noticing it as they drove past.

24

This was the yuppie era when everyone seemed to have money. As Poppy was an ex-working girl and a glamorous one at that, she had many connections. Sometimes groups of four to five guys would come in at once bringing champagne, cocaine and wads of cash: footballers, musicians and other well known people.

One time a well known footballer came in the late afternoon, got straight on to the Charlie and didn't leave until the next day. We all knew what he was like but he paid in hundreds so it didn't matter. He only had to make a phone call and his driver would turn up with more drink or whatever anybody wanted.

Visiting clients

After a bit I got fed up with working in saunas and I had heard a bit about going to visit clients or "outcalls" as it is known. I rang a number in a paper: The advertisement was simple - "Girls required" - so I rang up to find out all about it. It was quite a strange set-up really. Bill was a very well spoken guy on the other end of the phone and he told you he had to come to your house to interview you. That was how it worked. I wondered if he would expect me to show him what I could do. I heard later that that was his thing if he thought he could get away with it with certain girls. In my case it didn't happen. He liked me instantly. And he made me a lot of money.

How it worked was like this. A driver would come in the morning to collect you from your house and drive you to the base which was an old council flat in Kent. Everything was on a computer: names of clients, girls, everything. He was very clever, and remember that we were still in the '80s long before everyone had a computer at home. This meant he could run the visiting massage on his own.

One of his clever things was that when a client rang the number for a visiting massage he would think he was talking to a woman on the other end of the line. Bill was clever at that. You sat there while he checked out the client. If he felt that the client was OK, the driver would be waiting and off you would go.

While Bill was talking to the client he would make gestures so you would know what was going on. When the phone went he would ask the caller for his phone number. Then you would ring the number back on another line. If it was engaged he would know the client was ringing from that number and he would give the thumbs up sign. If it was ringing he would give the thumbs down. He would carry on talking in his sweet little voice and all of a sudden he would say "Can you wait a minute please". Then he would change voice and say "You're not ringing from that number are you, 'cause I've got a little machine that tells me you are not ringing from that number. Then bang, he puts down the telephone.

Nine out of ten times people checked out but some people slipped through the net. Sometimes he would leave other people in charge of doing the desk which is when slip-ups happened. "Oh, he did sound all right…Do you want to take a chance with him?"

The money that I had to pay was £10 for the driver, or £20 if it was further away, and £10 commission to Bill. So the moment you walked into the house you had to take that money to pay Bill and the driver. Anyway, I started doing three shifts a week of 12 hours or sometimes longer. I would make more money than I did in saunas but the hours were longer. The driver would pick me up at 10 in the morning but I could still have calls at midnight or one in the morning. Inevitably that type of client was always pissed or out of their head on coke.

The services I gave were the usual ones: full sex with a condom, a blowjob with a condom or wanking the man which can more politely be known as hand relief. The standard charge meant that you never left with less than £100 out of which you had to pay the driver and the agency. You had to make sure that your clients gave you £100 plus. Remember that it was in the 1980s so it was more like £200 in today's money.

Sometimes clients would ask for other services to satisfy their fantasies. A favourite is to be asked to do toe-sucking. It is not unusual for a guy to pay you £100 for just lying there to suck your toes and then you would try and wank him off with your feet. Also, many asked for a bit of caning or spanking. I'd say that when eight out of 10 clients have asked for that it has always been very mild like a mild form of domination. Now and then they would want to turn the whip on you but that's a matter of trust. There's a level you are willing to go to. Some girls are into it, some aren't. If a guy wanted to spank you then you could take another £40 off him to do that. If he wanted to give you six lashes, he'd give you £40. Forty quid just to

26

stand there and take six lashes, most girls could cope with that.

Another one that was sometimes asked for was water sports. You would find in those days it was probably the older guys who would ask for that. I had a few guys who were in their seventies, ex-army who would ask for those sorts of things. By today's standards, even younger guys like them. And today "hard sports" have come about in the last ten years. Hard sports are when they want you to shit on them and to eat your shit.

Getting clients to pay

When clients ask for extra services, generally you would take the money first. Normally you could suss the guy out in five or ten minutes. Sometimes you would come unstuck by being trusting and not getting the money up front and then getting knocked for the lot, but that's the way the game is. It's the same in all places: flats and saunas. Some clients do runners. They're not going to pay you but what can you do about it? You can't call the police. End of story. You just feel a bit gutted.

Anyway there was a lot of cash doing visiting massage. £1,000 a week or more. And I was still living at home as a single girl so I was rolling. I could do this job quite easily and cope with the hours. That's where I got the money together for cosmetic work on my teeth and I had fantastic holidays: the Seychelles, Barbados, wherever I wanted.

I also spent money on drugs. I managed to stay a recreational user and was never addicted. I've been able to stay that way. These days I occasionally share a spliff but never when I'm at work. As a rule I only do cannabis when I am stressed and otherwise I don't need it. I still smoke cigarettes, mainly roll-your-own and probably one day I'll manage to kick them.

I work regularly in a sauna now and none of the girls or clients do drugs in our shop. Saunas just about manage to keep the police away by being within the law but if you are raided and they find Class A drugs that would be the end of the shop concerned.

It was different when I was doing visiting massage. It wasn't that I had to go to a dealer and buy Coke. Coke was around a lot in the circle of clients who could afford upwards of £100 for an hour of my time. It's much the same today. It has always been around and always will be. In the '80s everyone had money. There were plenty of Jack-the-Lads: scrap metal dealers and yuppies and all sorts. It was all about champagne Charlie. You would go round to clients' houses in the middle of the afternoon. Some of them were very influential people. You would find lines of cocaine and be offered a drink. And that was three in the afternoon.

Then I would start thinking, God I'm getting out of my head already and I've still got the rest of the shift to do. Then sometimes they'd say "Here's a grand" and I would stay in for the rest of the day or another three to four hours with them. That was a relief because then I could be as high as a kite and pissed as well.

The client would always be told he'd get an hour, but your aim was always to get out in about 45 minutes if you could. Most clients would be OK but some would time you to the door. The best were the ones who would just say "Do what you've got to do" and then would let you go. In essence they wanted to get their orgasm and that was it.

Some clients just wanted you to get off your head with them. They wanted company, really. After a certain amount of coke and booze they frequently couldn't get it up anyway.

Working as a visiting girl had its advantages. It gave you more freedom and fantastic money. I had wonderful holidays and it felt good to be able to walk into a dentist with £5,000 to have all my teeth veneered. So though the life-style was good, it brought drugs and alcohol too.

You had to think about the drivers a bit, though. Some were good and some were bad. They wanted to get off with you but that didn't happen. Because I was being driven around I didn't have to worry about being high or pissed. But it took its toll. Some days you don't want even to get out of bed. So I used to have a few drinks at 11.00 in the morning and, what the hell, I'd lose my inhibitions. And that was when I first realised that my drinking was getting out of control. I was allowing it to happen and it was easy because I could just sit there and be driven around. The smarter girls drove so they were making the taxi money as well but I decided not to do the driving. It was too tiring and it was much easier for me to sit there being driven and drunk.

The first time I was raped

All of us girls, whether we work the street, the beat, the sauna, the club or the flat, we are all vulnerable. In a sauna you feel more secure. Clients are coming into your territory. On the other hand flats give me the creeps and always have. I hate working in flats. I've done it a few times when I desperately needed a bit of dough. Flats are not me. I find that the clientele in flats is different. Girls will tell you that clients who have girls visit them, clients who go to flats and clients who do saunas are all a little bit different.

I found that the clients who go to flats were cheaper, rougher, and still are. You are likely to get a lot more foreigners: Indians, Greeks and the like. It's not even a massage. All they want is a quick fuck. Most of them don't shower. And it's on a double bed. I find it seedy and cheap, and as you are rolling round on a bed they take liberties. They want to grope any part of you. They want to kiss you and that means French kissing. They want to sleep with you and make love with you but you are there to provide a service and not to roll around with a client paying you just £30 for a quick hand-relief. So I prefer to be in a massage room with a massage table. You are more in control.

Also I found that people behind flats are greedy. They want half your money and then you've got to pay the maid. Flats are never for me.

Visiting can also be dangerous and I had a really bad experience when I was raped. I was sent to a flat in Stratford. I hated going to Stratford or anywhere to do with East London. The clients were rough and gave aggravation. This particular job had bad vibes from the start. My driver pulled up outside a concrete jungle. I looked at him and said "I don't fancy this". I could see it was a high-rise block. The drivers were never allowed to be in view of the client so they couldn't walk you to the door or anything. They had to stay completely out of view.

I went up to this high-rise flat and knocked on the door. A black guy answered. My instincts said to me straight away I don't want to go in this front door at all, but I went in. The door got locked behind me but I kept cool. I realised very quickly that he was a Yardie. There was crack cocaine everywhere. It was clearly the kind of place you go to when you've done a job. Nobody lived there. Obviously they were keeping low for a few days. There was money everywhere and there were guns. I almost shat myself.

29

Then another guy appeared and I thought Oh my God! But I kept cool, I kept calm and just thought I've got to get out of here as fast as I can. They were talking amongst themselves and I said "Look, the boss at the agency says only one guy. I am not being funny, but I cannot massage both of you."

Another thing was that if you felt you were being intimidated you could let them know that the driver was outside. I would say, I'm going to have to tell my driver. I was trying to work a plan, but they weren't having it. They knew that if I walked out of that door, I wasn't coming back. They were high, they were sweating and they kept disappearing into the kitchen. I knew that they were doing the crack pipe there.

Then they came back and gave me money. By then they were getting even more worked up, hyped up and sweating. Then they raped me. There was nothing I could do about it. There was no point in screaming because I was frightened I might get shot, stabbed, hurt. You don't fuck about with Yardies especially when they are high on crack cocaine.

So I just let them do with me what they wanted. It felt I was in there a lifetime, but I was praying that if I let them do it I might just get out of there. And I did. I did manage to get away. When their buzz had gone down I just got my stuff together and I ran out of that place. Shoes in my hand I rushed down the stairs and got into the car screaming and crying. I took a long time off after that to recover and I never went back to visiting massage.

30

Chapter 5
BOSSES

I've had so many bosses over the years. Bosses were always on the lookout for new faces. Places go quiet from time to time and like many other girls I found myself working at two or three places at once. I would do a twelve hour shift in Essex, then travel to London the next day to do a shift standing in for someone else, followed by two days in a flat that I had heard was very busy. Working like this, it became a safe bet that I would earn a minimum £1,000 a week. Life was good and for the moment.

Madams

I see a difference between being boss of a sauna and being a madam. The main difference is the question of control. A madam lives by control and doesn't work anymore. She's probably been a working girl for some years and then she has found she can make a lot more money by hiring working girls. If she is a good businesswoman she can own several saunas, live in a big house and drive around in a flashy car. Madams are wealthy and ruthless. Their whole life is to do with the game. They live it, sleep it, drink it. It's their main priority in life. You'll find that madams go into it on a big scale. This means control over illegal girls. When the Thai girls were a big commodity they would be known to work for madams. It would be quite usual to have five Thai girls on one day in the sauna all being told by the madam that they have got to screw for £40 and pay the madam £20. To me, that's control.

Granted, the madams have to take the risk of having the police raid the sauna and holding them responsible. However a lot of the time they wouldn't be there and the girls would be told to say that they took all the money that the clients paid.

A boss is different. They lay down a few rules but your body is your body. They are not going to tell you how much you've got to charge to give any particular service and then take half your money.

I'm a boss myself now and I try not to squeeze my girls. If a girl has had a bad day, I would never take all the money from her. Just occasionally I have to squeeze, though. By contrast madams are ruthless. They want their money and they don't care about you.

In my shop the client pays a sum as soon as he comes in and that money goes straight to the shop. Supposing the sum is £15 for each client and the shop has just five clients in the day, you couldn't run a business on £75. So the girl pays part of the money she makes. In a decent shop the girl might pay £50 for the first client plus £20 for each one after that. If she does three clients at £60 she takes £180, pays £90 to the shop and takes home £90. That's not a lot for a 12 hour shift. With more clients you aim to go home with £150 upwards. That's by today's standards. What with the recession the sauna business today is not what it was ten or even five years ago. You can find yourself doing three shifts now and only earning the money you would have earned in one shift five or ten years ago.

When a girl leaves you ask your existing staff if they'd like to take her shifts on. If they don't want to you have to find new faces. There used to be plenty of girls flitting around just as I used to do, but now it's much harder. Even if you put an ad in the paper saying there's a vacancy in a sauna you may not get suitable girls. It's more common to get a girl from another sauna through word of mouth. In some areas, like the place where I have my sauna, you can't put ads in the local paper anyway.

Things have changed over recent years. There are still enough girls around wanting to do shifts but it's not like it used to be when girls would knock on the shop's door and ask if there were any shifts going. In the saunas I know, the boss is still a working girl and she treats the other girls in a friendly way. She tries to allocate the shifts so as to fit in with what the girls want. Many of them have families to look after and so they can only do one or two shifts a week. When school holidays come the girls have to change things around a bit and the boss has to give new shifts or bring in girls from outside. Human relations have to be thought about.

All girls have their regulars and they are pretty good about not poaching another girl's reg. But when a new client comes in he normally wants to see the girls on offer. If the boss gives shifts to a girl who is much younger or prettier she is going to get the new business and she will upset the girls who work there regularly. It's a competitive business being a working girl and good bosses have to treat their girls well.

32

The trend today is that girls are saying I might as well work for myself rather than pay the boss half my money. Bosses have got greedier and greedier. They've got girls working in flats with the bosses taking half their money. They get away with it in the case of foreign girls because many don't have visas. So the boss has control like it used to be years ago. Exploiting working girls is becoming part of the underworld again along with drugs and organised crime.

Every shop has a book in which the girls record the names that the clients give them. Most clients make these up on the spot and John is the one that many new clients give. The name doesn't matter but keeping the book right is important. Most shops have CCTV at the entrance now so a madam or a boss can check on how many clients came each day. If they are good at running the place they won't need to do much of that but anyway the cameras are essential in case any weirdoes or creeps try to get in and give the girls grief.

Inevitably there is the temptation that if you know your boss is away for the day, you would think that s/he wouldn't notice if some clients weren't recorded. The girls get to know each other quickly and if they both ignored what the other was at, just a couple of clients knocked from the book would be enough to leave another £100 or more in their purses at the end of the day.

Most working girls like to think of themselves as honest, at least to a certain degree. But whether they have worked for whomsoever — their friends, the agencies, their best friends even — I think we all have knocked the shop sometimes.

Madam X

One of my early bosses was Madam X. She had been a working girl who had set up on her own. As well as doing shifts I found that there were additional things I would get involved with. I wasn't forced or even pressured but I went along with it all. Some nights one or two of the other girls and I would all go to a wine bar, get shitfaced, and go back to a client's lovely pad in Hertfordshire where we would chill out till the morning.

Madam X, who liked her coke, would often turn up just before closing time at the sauna on a high. She would be wearing the latest designer clothes, her hair done at a trip to the hairdresser. In her bubbly, working-mode voice she would say, "Hi, babe, how you doing? I'm off to the West End tonight. Fancy coming, Eliana?" Sometimes I'd say yes. What the hell! There were always plenty of guys and plenty of C around if she was at the party.

Madam X was clever and within two years she had three other places. I would work a shift or two at all the places. Maybe one was busier than the others, and believe you me, when you sit in a place with no windows or natural light, twelve hours are a long time. On a bad day maybe you've only seen one client. Still, you had to do that to get a good shift another time in the busiest sauna.

It was not unusual to leave one place and go back many times. Familiar haunts familiar jaunts. Some girls moved around a lot but mainly they were the ones who had complicated lives with pimps, children and drugs or who were trying to run from something. I was one who liked a settled place and building up a list of regular clients so that I knew roughly who was coming in and how much I would be taking home. Establishing myself in one place worked for me.

I left Madam X around 1987. It was getting tougher. The more successful she became, the more rules she would make. She became controlling. If a client came in at 11.00 in the evening she would make you do him even though more than likely he would be out of his head. The other girls would have gone home, so it was just the client, me and the greedy boss. These were the moments that depressed me: sitting in a steaming hot Jacuzzi at midnight with a drunk man poring over you and probably wanking under the bubbles. At least the humidity hid my tears. Times like these would find me detouring on the way home to get some drugs, get wrecked and forget about everything. The next day the only comfort was the money and I would spend every penny. It felt like solace.

Another sauna I worked in was like a breath of fresh air. It was modern and friendly and run by a very buxom blonde whose boyfriend was an East End gangster. In fact most places were run by these men. The woman in charge was normally the front for the place: in other words the one who took the shit in police raids. The men behind it were always safe.

She smiled a lot and I remember staring at her silicone enhanced breasts thinking she must make a fortune with those. What an asset! That's why so

34

many working girls had boob jobs.

As soon as I came along she took one look at me and asked how many shifts I would like to do. Each sauna owner would give you a brief rundown on prices and how the place was run. Madam Bigboob's place was swinging with rock stars, soap stars and lords. One of them was known as the poser. He would come in and pose in the big mirror in his white Y-fronts. We were paid to stand round and watch him and then wank him off.

The ex-working girl bosses were and always will be the worst because they know all the tricks that are pulled. Ruthless, hard and cunning, they forget very quickly what it's like to sit on the other side of the fence. Many women bosses soon become enemy Number One. Not much gets past a woman boss. They know that some of the girls will try to "knock the shop" by not registering a client as he comes in. That way she gets to keep all the cash she takes off him and she doesn't contribute to the shop's overheads. It just boils down to the fact that it is a woman's business after all.

Male bosses

Male bosses come from all walks of life: from the villain to the working-class man with an ordinary day job. The ones who think they can make a fast buck out of working girls know fuck-all about the business. I'd like a pound for every man who has said to me "I'd do the same if I was a bird". I've always said that a man's body isn't big enough for tenderness and testosterone.

When your boss was a villain you knew where they were coming from but when Joe Bloggs who has visited saunas gets glamorous ideas about owning his own place with sexy girls and lots of money, in reality he hasn't a clue and just wants to get into your knickers for free. At least when you worked for a big man you were safe and guaranteed to earn money. Because of their status you would never be under pressure for sexual favours. Villains were far above that. They just saw you as a money machine and if you gave them a little more it was a bonus for them. Their main concern was that you were beautiful and good at your job.

I worked for some great people and one boss in particular will always stick in my mind. He was a multi-millionaire with a heart who had helped so many girls over the years, including me, get mortgages, loans and cars. He was part of the underworld and had made his money in the '70s through property and prostitution. Although ruthless in business he was a kindly man with a million dollar smile who made you feel at ease. He wanted every working girl to do well. He wanted you to live your life, enjoy your money and to move on to better things. He was always willing to help you as he had many connections.

One time I was in serious trouble with the Inland Revenue and he took me to an accountant somewhere in Essex. He was an eccentric man, but what the hell, I gave him £500 and my tax was sorted.

These were the kind of people you needed to know. I was soon selected to work for Mr Big in the West End. If you got a shift in his place you were tops. I was one of the few girls from his various saunas in Essex to get the chance to work there. Lucky me!

Most of the other male bosses I worked for were more or less OK: clever and drawn by money. Some lived in big houses and had the whole thing sussed and some were just dirty pervs with big drug addictions to match. Those ones were ugly and unappealing to women in every sense. Luckily, as I was lovely and good at the game I could move away very quickly from those types.

When massaging I would always hear the one about "my mate is thinking about opening up a place like this" and I would think, here we go again. Another wanker who thinks that I would be remotely interested in his sleazy offer while I am wanking him off. What planet are they on, I would ask myself. They are just looking for sex for free.

Male bosses are a lot different from female bosses or madams for one obvious reason: they haven't done the business.

There are different sorts of male bosses. One of them is the guy who sets up a sauna thinking it is a good way to make a fast buck. Some of them would think that he would get to fuck all the girls as well. These guys would hope that it was going to be a nice career for them. Better than being a taxi-driver.

And then you got the other type: the villains who were part of the underworld who had their fingers in many other pies. Actually these were

36

the best ones to work for because you knew you were safe. You know you are looked after in a funny sort of way. Their places are usually busy because they are run right. They've got money so if the shower doesn't work it gets fixed quick because they know the plumbers, the electricians. They know everybody.

The amateurs, the taxi-drivers aren't good to work for because they don't know how to run the place. I've answered adverts and walked into someone's place and saw some guy sitting there with a dog eating off a plate. He's running this little operation from a council flat and he's probably a really nice guy. So you may be willing to come and see him and have a joint but he's not going to get you much money. And some of these guys really don't know what's going on so some of the girls go in there and take the piss.

The Big Guy bosses were part of the underworld and had links with the Bill. I was friendly and the Big Guys were kind to me. I had respect for them, not just because of their money and power. They were good to their working girls and helped me at times along the way by giving me good jobs in good shops, encouraging me to pay my taxes, persuading me in a good way to play half straight. I know where a few of them still live and it is intriguing and fun to drive past their big houses with walls and gates. I always look and smile and slow down. If I am ever spotted I always get a wave, a wink, a hug and on the odd occasion a kiss.

Unless you are one of the Big Guys, the bottom line is that it's a woman's business, not a man's. You'll find that the East End villains aren't in there hassling you. They are away. Their dolly-birds are on the door and on reception. So the villains are on the case but they're not in your face. They are just there to make money. They are not even likely to ask for favours for free. That comes more from the other guys in the business. But it has been known that the villains get to have affairs with some of the classy girls. I've not been under pressure from the villains to give a sexual favour and if I did it on a few occasions I was paid. It was never taken for granted.

Women bosses

Though I always say that the business is a women's business, the best bosses I have worked for have been men. Most women bosses have played the game and been in the business as working girls themselves and have

37

then branched out on their own. They know the tricks and the scams. They are bitchy and greedy. They don't give you any slack. A man boss can walk into the shop to collect the shift money and you can tell him you've had a bad day or whatever, He may be sympathetic but a woman boss won't put up with that. She wants her money, she wants her cut. They aren't necessarily bad, but they are hard. If they've been working girls themselves who have set up their own little place, that's all they've got and they want to make it pay. Men may have their fingers in other pies as well.

The main scam that women bosses watch out for is when girls don't write down the clients they have had. If the shop doesn't have cameras and the client is in and out quickly it's easy to knock the shop by "forgetting" to record him. Your male bosses are more likely to accept that nobody has been in. The female boss will simply say she doesn't believe it for the simple reason that they have done it themselves.

Mind you the boss can fire a working girl from a sauna like from any other job. It's much easier in fact. No redundancy pay or employment tribunals for working girls. Girls can get fired if they don't do enough clients. If a girl is reliable she may turn up 10 minutes before the shift and stay to the last dot but she may be no good for business. Then you have another girl who turns up an hour late but who brings in the clients. She may also be taking clients to her own private place. She may leave an hour early. The boss has to choose. Generally she prefers the reliable girl but at the end of the day it comes down to how much money each girl makes for the shop.

Some bosses don't want any drugs in the place. In the past drugs were part and parcel of the sauna scene. Bosses didn't mind if a girl was stoned provided the clients kept coming and she was putting money on the table. Things vary according to the boss and the local police force. Everyone knows that the term "sauna and massage" when it is advertised means a knocking shop or, as the press would say, a brothel. If the place has drugs going on there it would be easy for the police to raid it and get it closed down for trading in drugs. In my place the girls aren't allowed to do drugs and the police know that it is clean. I've had officers come round and tell me that so long as we keep clean from drugs they won't bother us. My place has been there for 30 years and we don't expect trouble. Personally I would fire a girl if she flaunted using drugs. What girls do with clients when they are in the room is down to them but they've got to keep it away from me.

38

Jimmy – a good boss

Other than word of mouth working girls used to find jobs through newspaper ads in the personal column. It is very different now when most papers ban these. If you wanted somewhere completely different that's where we would look. At that time even the *Evening Standard* would let saunas advertise though mostly it was for hostess jobs in the West End. Occasionally you would see an ad: "masseuse required".

On one occasion I decided: "Let's go for it". After all it was in the *Evening Standard* and it was a London number. I wanted somewhere my other work associates and I hadn't yet ventured. A Scottish accent said "Hello, Jimmy speaking". Straight away I felt this guy was kind of sound and maybe a little more as sauna bosses don't answer their phones in such a professional manner. I liked his voice straight away and we had a brief conversation beginning with me saying "Hi, I saw your ad". But soon it became apparent to me that I was interviewing him, not the other way round.

He told me honestly over the telephone that this was a new venture for him and a pal of his. Usually if someone is so blunt as to tell you all that straight away you would stay well clear. You would think that this was another idiot trying to live off women and as the guy doesn't know what he is doing you would be the one responsible for making the place busy. If you wanted to stay there you would have to build it up, get regulars and work hard. If the guy gave a hint that he was new to all this, you would know it was a no-no. Also I needed money and fast. I didn't have time to sit there building up someone's place when I needed money right now. But I did need a change and that change was to become a challenge.

I met Jimmy the following evening. I didn't drive in those days. I don't know if I was stupid or just too trusting but I gave him my mum's address and told him to ring me when he was outside. True to each other's word we met at the next turning to my mum's house. He was driving a Y series BMW. He had a very warm, laid-back Scottish accent. I liked this guy instantly even if I found him hard to understand. He was funny, with a very dry sense of humour. And there was me, young, pretty and ready for my next mission. So far he had been blind-eyed to the sauna world and he didn't seem the sort of guy who would have connections or even consider getting into it for any reason. He was new to the business and I knew the business well. It was a case of him wanting to help me and me wanting to

39

help him. For him it was to be a new adventure. Anyway, I liked him and he liked me.

He had taken on a sauna in Surrey, and true to his word he picked me up the following day and he took me from Essex to the sauna. He did this five days a week for a long time. The sauna was a going concern but it had run down. He had taken it over from a friend. By the time I came on the scene there was only one girl working there. Jimmy came in to try and turn it round and save the place. Basically he was starting off blind and he was starting off with me. He took me up to the shop and I felt comfortable with it. It was small. I liked the idea of working for Jimmy. He didn't seem pushy. He wasn't trying to get hold of me or shag me. He was different and it was a new adventure for me. I needed to prove to him that if you get girls like me who you can trust, you can make money. I can build your place up, trust me.

He also told me that he had interviewed another girl. She happened to be black and she was lovely, and I am mixed race. I realised then how naïve this guy was. He wanted the two of us to work in his sauna five, six, seven days a week. She was a lovely girl, though scatty as arse-holes. She and I got on very well and it struck us very quickly that he didn't have clue because you wouldn't start up a sauna with two black girls seven days a week. But our personalities clicked and, believe you me, personality is a key factor in building up a sauna business. You take for granted that the girls have to be pretty with good legs and slim figures, but then it is their personality that attracts the client in the first place. If you get it right it turns him into a regular. Within six months we turned the place round. Anyway Jimmy continued to pick me up and drive me both ways to the sauna.

To begin with the place was slow. I would only see one or two clients a day but it was better than nothing because I needed some income. As he picked me up each day and took me home I had no travel costs. He was always a gentleman. Initially he didn't even take money off me. He didn't know what the usual set-up was and if I only did one or two clients, he knew that wasn't a lot of money. Even when I was earning good money and of course by then we were paying him shift money, he still wouldn't take any extra from me for driving me. Jimmy was a good guy.

From this experience I learned that I have the personality that builds up numbers at a place. A lot of bosses have benefitted from that. I am very good at it and all bosses knew that about me. In Jimmy's case I had to start a place almost from scratch and that was the challenge. I stayed with him for a couple of years and became close friends with Carol, the black girl. We did five days a week together, Monday to Friday, and to begin with we covered weekends too, one of us at a time. Then he got another girl for the weekends. Between us we made the place grow from one or two for each girl to five or six or eight. If you have done eight clients in a shift you have had a really good day. When the place reaches that point you need to bring in other staff and girls so that the shop can work properly.

One day a new girl came to the shop. She was a beautiful, beautiful Irish girl. Jimmy made the mistake of getting involved with her. This meant that his marriage went funny and things became complicated. At the same time it seemed that Jimmy was losing interest in the shop. We came to understand that he wasn't the main owner of the business. There was a bigger guy behind him, someone called Kenny of Irish descent. He was a very respected man in the area: a multi-millionaire who owned the building. He was just as nice a guy as Jimmy. I met him quite often. Even though he owned the place he never tried to use his money and power to get at the girls.

I remember one incident to show what sort of man he was. I personally lost some money: in fact a £50 note. We thought it was the receptionist because she was only on £50 a night and she was planning to get married, but in fact it was one of the girls who were working with me that night. Kenny heard about the incident and he came round next day. He gave me an envelope. In it were two £50 notes.

Because Jimmy wasn't the ultimate owner he personally wasn't making much money so he decided to bring another guy in to run the business: a nephew or a cousin. He was a young guy: flash, cocky and 20 years old. The minute he came in the door I took an instant dislike to Danny. He was green, he didn't have a clue, he thought he was fantastic and behind him in tow he had his beautiful little blonde. And they thought they were going to come in there and tell all of us girls what to do and what not to do, and they thought they were going to live a good life off us. He had taken on another place in Harrow and he told Carol and me that we had to move there. We simply told him we just weren't doing it, so that is how we both came to leave.

Harry - another good boss

One man I worked for was a bit different. It was in my early days when I had been doing nursing and also had been on a few escort dates for an agency in the West End. It was a time when I had been a bit depressed and sometimes didn't bother to turn up for a date fixed by the agency.

The circumstances of meeting Harry were rather funny. This time the agency sent me to a hotel in the Edgware Road. It may have been the Metropole. Accidentally I walked into the wrong hotel which was the building immediately before it. It wasn't a proper hotel. It was bed-sits. I remember thinking this isn't a posh hotel. I went up a flight of stairs and there is a room with a little man sitting at the table. Black hair, gold rim glasses, rather hyper. He had a suit on but he was a sweaty short man.

I soon realised that the place was used by working girls by the way he approached me. I said the name of the man I was supposed to go and see, thinking it might be him. He started flustering, and there was someone else in the room with him who he sent out. Then he said:

"Are you working?" I told him the name of the hotel I was looking for and he said "It's not this one. It's the next one, but sit down. I thought you were a girl who was going to bring a client in because some working girls do rent rooms here. I do operate some girls here myself".

So within ten minutes he was asking me to work for him. Me being naïve and late for the booking anyway I decided there and then not to go to the proper hotel for the appointment. So instead Harry and I were sitting there having a drink and a chat. Harry was middle-aged and I felt he was kinky but I liked him. And he wasn't trying to have it on with me.

Anyway, we swapped phone numbers and he said if I'd come in on Friday at 11.00 a.m. he would have a room for me and he would send clients up to me. I liked the idea of men coming to me and not me having to tramp round hotels getting lost, getting into the wrong lifts and getting chucked out. I get all paranoid about that sort of thing. So I liked the idea.

So a few days later I did turn up there. I walked up the stairs and Harry and his son were there. What a good-looking guy the son was! Tall and handsome. Harry took me up to a room and he asked me if I would let

42

another girl lick my pussy. I'm thinking: "where are the clients?" Then he went on: "I don't want to have sex with you. I don't want to have sex with any of the girls. But upstairs there is a little black girl. Her thing is that I get her girls for her to lick."

It all seemed a bit bizarre but I wanted work.

Harry goes upstairs and he comes down and he says: "Have a little freshen up" while I was still thinking, is this for real? I sit on the bed and within minutes Harry is back with a little black girl. She was funny looking and she reminded me of a jazz singer. Jet black with Afro hair and very plain, very quiet, she hardly spoke. She looks at Harry and he nods. "Go on, it's all right". To me he says: "go on, just lie there".

Meanwhile I could see that Harry was touching himself in his trousers. I lay there on the bed with my legs apart with the black girl licking my pussy. That was my very first experience. To be honest I wanted to laugh because at that time I hadn't even had much experience of men doing it because I was that young. Anyway I remember putting my hands on her head, on her Afro, and she was loving it. I think I enjoyed it but I was young, about 19. It wasn't what I had gone there for. I had stumbled on Harry by accident anyway and I remember lying there thinking, bloody hell, your son's good looking. He was in the office lower down but he must have known what was going on.

It was all a bit funky and I kept thinking why is it happening and what am I doing? But I did it because I was thinking "Harry's going to get me work". And there was Harry in there wanking off. That was his thing. He said "I'll never hurt you, I'll never shag you. I don't do anything with my girls. I'll never pressure you ever. But that's what I like to watch. He used to do the same with the other girls. After that he got me quite a few clients. I stayed for four or five months.

One time Harry set me up with a guy in St John's Wood. He was an Arab and I hated him. I went to him a few times and I'd say to Harry I don't like him because he is rough. He stank of BO but he was rich. Harry would say, just get his fucking money. We were talking of £130 and I'd give Harry £30. One night I went to the Arab and the condom split on me. I remember saying "I'm never fucking coming here again". I went back to the bedsit crying my eyes out and Harry was wonderful. He said "I'm going back to

43

get some more fucking money out of him for you". And he did. He told the Arab that I'd have to go up to the clinic, do this, do that because the condom burst. And if she's fucking pregnant I'll want some money out of you." He got in his car with me, drove straight to St John's Wood and he got more money from the Arab. He was always on the girl's side.

Harry used to say to me: you're young, you're beautiful. Come and see me now and then but fucking stop doing this. Look at all them fucking scag-heads who rent my rooms (his word for the girls who did heroin). Go and do something with your life. You are a mess.

You could trust Harry. He was lovely and you felt safe when you were there because he was always within earshot. If a client raised his voice he would be up in the room.

That burst condom with the Arab did actually stop me in my tracks for quite a time.

Chapter 6
BOYFRIENDS, PARTNERS, GIRLFRIENDS AND FRIENDS

Working girls' relationships with men are always difficult. I know to my cost. My relationship with Max, who comes later, was terrible and my other relationships have come unstuck. Part of the trouble lies in my mind. Here I am, a working girl for 20 years. I'm in a stable relationship now but I'm still plagued by doubts. I guess that out of ten men who come to see me about eight are cheating on a partner. Some of them are open about it and say so. Sometimes they say they no longer get on with the partner. Sometimes they say that they still care for her but she is no good in bed. Either way you know that if the partner found out there would be tears. And here I am as a working girl making it all possible. For the ones who are genuinely single coming to see me is a good way to get sex and it must be better than wanking because otherwise why would they pay quite a lot of money for it? But that leaves the other eight men who are cheating on their partners.

Looking at things in a different way I try to imagine how I would feel if my boyfriend were to tell me one day that he'd had been to see a sauna girl like me. Or worse still if he didn't tell me and I found out. I'd feel sick, absolutely devastated. I'd feel the same way if he was screwing any girl and no money was involved.

For me these are two different issues. I think that ordinary women think that going to a working girl is the lowest thing her partner can do. I happen to think that it's better to pay money and have no emotional involvement rather than screwing some woman who then gets emotionally tangled. Men that visit saunas categorically don't come in looking for an affair. In the sauna no emotional attachments are intended but as we have to be bubbly and friendly all the time, some clients may imagine that we really like them. In fact it's just the way we do our job.

My difficulty is that I am a one-on-one person and I would like to be that way but so long as I am working girl I find it difficult to reconcile that with my life-style. Despite my many bad experiences and my need to be

45

independent, I'm a sensitive girl. And of course men are so different from women. They can fuck without emotion. I see that several times a day every day of my working life.

I'm one of those women who when I'm outside the sauna I can't fuck without emotion. To give my heart and soul to a man I have to love him and be in love with him so that I am emotionally attached. So I have this conflict in my mind. I do my job as a working girl but the thought of my partner seeing a girl in the middle of the afternoon blows my mind. And yet I'm helping other men do that all day long.

Personally I am lucky to have a guy who doesn't take my money, doesn't beat me, doesn't pimp me or call me a whore or bad names. Even in bad arguments he never throws it in my face and never has.

Then the other side to it is this. Can a man truly love you if he can accept what you do for a living? Does it give him the right to a free rein and to have sex with other women? Or do they want to have their cake and eat it?

It's my job that makes me feel insecure about those things. I've got worse as I've got older. I've noticed it becoming stronger. It's a barrier now which is becoming stronger and stronger and I'm finding it harder to deal with. It's frustration because I want to get out of the business.

It's strange, maybe ironic to think that I've been in the business on and off since I was fifteen. I chose to be a working girl and have always treated the sex business in all its variations as something which was there, something that paid good money, and now I'm drawing back from it. All that time I didn't have any qualms about giving clients the services they want. Yet now I find myself thinking that if all men were as honest and faithful as I would like my partner to be I wouldn't have a job except for the genuinely single men who are in a small minority. I'm having to confront that now. I think that some working girls can compartmentalise it all but I just can't. Men are much better at compartmentalising than women.

Men can say: I support my wife and kids, I put a roof over my family, I put food on the table, I have quality time with them and yes I love them. But sex is something I absolutely need and I'm not getting it from my wife so I go off and get it somewhere else. Maybe I feel guilty but I can compartmentalise. That's the man's way of doing it.

Trouble is I know that most men can do that, so why should my partner be different? It's very strange. I've been giving my body all my working life and for me it's just a service, it's my job. And like lots of other people in all walks of life I want to get out of my job. Yet the thought of my partner going to a working girl to get the things I do every day screws me up. I know it's very irrational but people aren't always rational. Women aren't and I'm not. That's all I can say.

Jayden, my first partner

For a working girl to have boyfriend is quite difficult. To begin with, the hours we work don't fit in with those of other people. More importantly, there is the question of how and when to tell a boyfriend about the job that we do. In the early stages of going out with a guy I can always disguise the truth. I can say I work in a beauty parlour or that I do modelling or I work as a carer. In fact I have done all those things so it is quite easy for me to pull the wool over the boyfriend's eyes. But it can't go on indefinitely. Also, having to lie right from the start of a relationship isn't a good way to go.

The second stage is when I tell the boyfriend what I really do. This is difficult. Most men have fixed ideas that girls shouldn't be doing sex for money and they are always likely to get jealous. They don't like the idea of sharing their girl with any guy who walks off the street into the sauna or the flat. Still less do they like the idea of visiting massage because of the risk entailed. So when I break the truth to a new boyfriend it takes courage on my part because it risks breaking the relationship. Often the boyfriend tells the girl to stop working but that doesn't solve the fact that she needs the money to live on. If the boyfriend is really in love with her he may suggest that they live together and he will support her. Two can live more or less for the same price as one, some people say. That may be true for paying the rent on a flat but it doesn't provide the basic things of life that I need. Apart from anything else, I became a working girl because I liked good clothes and a high standard of living. All that isn't easy to give up. Both the man and the working girl have to be very much in love to find a solution.

When I was still in my mid 20s I got involved with a guy called Jayden and we fell in love. He was a few years younger than me. He was also of mixed race. He had Mexican Indian blood which gave him dark skin, black hair and dark brown eyes. He loved me unconditionally. I never told him what I

47

did but I'll always swear he guessed or knew the truth and he loved me so much that it didn't matter. I was his world and our relationship was passionate. We were young, we went out most nights to nightclubs, ate good food and I had nice clothes. I told him that I was modelling which I had done a brief stint of in my earlier days. I had a terrific portfolio so when I told him I was a model he believed me because he wanted to believe me.

When our baby, a son, came along things changed inevitably. I had plenty of money saved up and I spent a lot on the baby. I spent £20k revamping our home and bought designer clothes for baby Ben. But though I was a new mum, I wasn't a normal mummy. I was still a working girl. No six weeks let alone six months maternity leave for me. No quality time that women normally enjoy. My time was only borrowed. I didn't breast feed Ben so that I could go back to work. I started working again in saunas within six weeks.

My relationship with Jayden lasted eight years and in many ways it was a good one. I loved him and I felt safe with him. In fact I think he idolised me more than I idolised him. He knew I worked but he never questioned it, ever. My photographs as a model enabled me to play that role but he always knew there was something else. Even when I was doing 12 hour shifts in saunas and was on the drugs scene and would come home all blasted or from a party, it was still OK. From his side, he would want to go out with his mates so neither of us complained and we accepted the other the way they were.

After a bit though, the relationship was beginning to get a bit tense. I had some friends in America and I went over there for a six week break in Miami to be away from him, away from everything. I went for six weeks just to see if I would miss him. My friends had gone to the US a few years earlier and were settled there. I met a lot of good people and had wonderful dreams about going back. I met some rich guys from New York who were on vacation. I actually had a job lined up to go back to, working at a yacht club. Something completely different and not as a working girl. The person I was staying with was an ex-working girl so I knew it could be done. She had made good and had children to support. There were none of the state benefits as in England. She had a nanny who she brought with her from the UK and who I knew very well. We used to spend the days together talking, so I could see how all these things could work out.

48

At the end of the six weeks I flew back. I realised how much I missed Jayden and I fell pregnant straight away. It was an unintended pregnancy. I hated the Pill which made me fat and spotty so I had a coil fitted. Contraception wasn't as advanced then as it is today. I never used condoms with Jayden.

At that time I was still living with my mum. When I fell pregnant it wasn't really a shock and I think I even knew the night it happened. It made a decision for me. When I came back from America there was a job lined up for me over there, somewhere to reside. I'd have had to apply for a green card but I could have stayed six weeks. That decision was taken away from me. So I just accepted it and thought, OK, this is what I am going to do now.

Jayden was over the moon about the baby. But I had to do with the fact that I was pregnant and I was working. I did have some money put by and was looking to buy my own place. I was still with my mum and I needed to get out. Then everything seemed to happen all of a sudden. I had a very good boss at the time, a very influential guy who was big in the West End. He knew everybody. If you wanted a driving licence or a mortgage or to deal with the Revenue, he could get it done. He was out to help me. I found a property I liked. I thought I could do it all. Get a mortgage, buy the house, have my man, have the baby. It was all going on and it looked so good, just like the perfect dream.

I put down a deposit of £15 grand for the mortgage. I walked into a solicitor's in Epping High Road with £15 grand in a bag. I can remember that day very well. It was a lovely Georgian-style house. An accountant made up some books for me to satisfy the Revenue. I paid a little bit of tax so everything looked sorted.

But then I came to see that I was more advanced, more mature than Jayden was. I was twenty-seven. He was three to four years younger but it seemed more than that. Like eight years, maybe. From my point of view it wasn't too early to have a child. I'd had quite a bit of life already.

Then the pressure got to him. The mortgage payments were high but as I was earning £500 per week I could afford £800 a month. But working when I was pregnant became quite different. It was disgusting and made me feel sick. It was partly that being pregnant makes you feel sick but also it brought home to me that this isn't how I see myself. You are meant to be pregnant, you are meant to be in love with someone but I am not meant to be here in a sauna. Having men mauling my breasts that were sore and looking at my bump made me all self-conscious. I felt nasty, I felt dirty, but I had a mortgage to pay.

And Jayden was lazy. He was still going out with his mates and in his heart of hearts he knew about my big bucks as well. It's hard for a man to get off his arse and earn a wage when he knows that somewhere there are big bucks. He may have been a kept man, but that's not a ponce or a pimp. I would never call him that but if he had his fags, his spliff and a fiver in his pocket for the day he was happy. He had jobs, on and off, in security.

When I had the house and was pregnant I got possessive with him and jealous especially when I did give up work. I'd gone through all my savings paying the mortgage and I had a breakdown. I had him followed one night. I was getting nutty with him and then I lost my house. That was a little while after the baby came. The baby went to stay with his grandparents for a bit. I went to a psychiatric hospital for a while. Close friends had to take over my house and sort out all the paperwork. I had letters from the Revenue, the mortgage company and the rest. I didn't know what was going on, I couldn't deal with it, but those people close to me helped me tremendously. They sorted everything out and even paid for things and solicitors, for which I am forever in their debt. And I went back and lived with my mum.

Most of the days that I spent in my dream house were filled with feeding the baby and me drinking. On one occasion I had got through a bottle of brandy before two in the afternoon. On another day I collapsed on the floor beside the Moses basket. My lovely, lovely neighbour next door who had a key to my house heard the baby crying for quite a while, knew something had happened, let herself in and called an ambulance. I was rushed to hospital where they found my liver was severely damaged by alcohol. I stayed in the hospital for two weeks and I was the colour of a banana. I was told when I came round that I was very lucky to be alive.

At that time Jayden and I were very volatile. Off, on, off, on, one day off, one day on. He couldn't commit. That was the problem. And post-natal depression kicked in on me. I'd lost my house, I'd got no money, I'd got a baby, I looked ill, I looked tired. And when I did go back to work I was zombified for a couple of years. I was just trying to pick myself up. I couldn't get used to being a mum. It took a couple of years before I felt like me again. I didn't look for talking therapy at the time. I felt I had to deal with things on my own and I'm still a bit like that. I'm dark in that respect. I need to deal with my own shit. I'm not the person to offload on a stranger. I get too agitated.

The trouble was as the years went on Jayden and I both took our relationship for granted. As I got more involved with work he went out more and more with his mates. Eventually I took a job in another sauna and moved on. But life had changed and I had changed. I'd lost a home, I had had an on-off relationship and gained a son — a real responsibility. I was broke, a single mother and with no place to call home. And this was my first taste of what it is like to be in debt. I've been in debt ever since then.

Looking back, Jayden was the first true love of mine and we are still friends. However, although Ben is Jayden's son Jayden never does anything for him. There is no relationship. He does nothing for me financially either but I am still fond of him. I am in touch with him now and then but that's it.

Max, the bastard I lived with

The difference between a boss and pimp is clear. Both of them want to make money out of you but a pimp is a guy who goes out looking for clients and then takes your money. Pimps are men whereas female bosses and madams have mainly been working girls themselves. They know the ups and downs of being a working girl so they should be a bit understanding. Pimps just look on girls as meat to make money for them. It's got to be sexy-looking, attractive meat and the girl should work hard at it to provide money for both of them. In essence, a pimp is a parasite who lives off a working girl.

Unfortunately for me I got mixed up with a bastard who lived off me for three years. He wasn't a pimp in the sense of finding clients for me, but he was a parasite who used me and my money to fund his own lifestyle and in particular his crack cocaine habit. He was the worst bastard I have ever known. Unfortunately I fell in love with him. I didn't see him coming. He saw me coming.

At the time I was working at a place in London. It belonged to one of the

51

big bosses. If you were good enough you were selected and taken from the sauna in Essex to the one in London. To get a shift there was like gold dust. We had all sorts of people coming in. In Essex we had sellers coming in: heisters, people nicking things and selling their gear on. In the West End they were selling better things. Every time the doorbell went it was somebody with diamond rings. Completely different things from what the heisters in Essex brought. The goods were more elaborate and classy.

And one day this bastard came in asking if anyone was interested in some gold jewellery. He was known in there. One of those faces that pops up now and then. I was new and he spotted me. I looked at him and thought he was a client but the receptionist said, "Oh no, he's got something to sell". He looked at me like he was saying, who is she? I looked at him. The receptionist called me over and said, "This is Max. He gets bits and pieces of jewellery".

Max got talking to me nicely. There was something about him, a magnet you could say that drew me towards him. He had that Mediterranean look. His hair was tied back in a long pony tail. He was smart, well suited. But he was the biggest bastard conman I was ever to meet in my life. I got sucked in. At the time I was looking for excitement. And I sure got some excitement from him for the next three years. I was 28 when it began.

The trouble was I was on the rebound from Jayden. I had little Ben and my mum was looking after him. I somehow was getting back to where I used to be and how I used to feel. I didn't think of it like that at the time but now I know I was on what people call the rebound. Max was good looking and he seemed exciting compared with Jayden. It looked like he had lots of money. Yes, he was a bit of a ducker and diver but he had style and class. That's what I thought. He looked at me and I looked at him and we both thought we looked like a glamorous couple together.

He sussed out that I was an East End girl who wore my heart on my sleeve. I was the soft touch. As I found out later he was married to a Jamaican girl. Jamaican girls are a tough lot who don't put up with any shit so he was used to the tough black side. So he saw me, a nice mixed race girl, as his little queen who he could twist round his finger. I fell for him because he was good looking, he said all the right things, he paid me attention and he took me out and gave me good sex.

I did find out early into the relationship that he was doing crack cocaine. I had taken cocaine and marijuana but I not been introduced to crack cocaine and I didn't understand the drug.

Six months into the relationship I discovered he was married. But I had fallen for him. I even set up home with this guy and he lived there with me and I still didn't realise he was married. The way he would live his life, he would tell his wife he was going on business in Birmingham. His wife had always known that sort of life-style. She was used to him being away for three days. He would then be with me for a few days and he would be telling me the same thing: "I'm going to Birmingham". I didn't realise how he worked. It was all new to me.

After he met me in the sauna, it was me who was giving him presents. I think I was trying to justify being a working girl. I was looking for him and me to live together, get money and set up home but I realised that though I was thinking that way, he was thinking another way. I foolishly let him know that I had quite a large sum of money put by. He got through it.

I also fell pregnant. This was before I found out he was married. He said there was no possible way I could have the baby because he was married. I was deeply disappointed, hurt. But even so the kind of way he lived his life excited me and I was adamant that I wasn't going to get rid of the baby.

But it made us split up for a bit. I realised that Max was a bastard. He would hit me and put some terrible bruises on my face. And worse.

Max didn't like baby Ben and I realised very quickly he wasn't going to give me that family unit. Baby Ben was being brought up by my mum. When I was with Max and Ben, Max would make very clear he didn't like Ben. He would make fun of Ben or else he would ignore us completely and piss off for a couple of days. Then he would ask me when I was taking Ben back to mum. Foolishly again and thanks to my wonderful mum, in my quest for love I went with Max and more or less gave Baby Ben to my mum.

But then I was learning more things about him. Looking back it should have been quite simple. I should have gone and got an abortion and never have spoken to Max again. But he had got into me. He gave me excitement. He took me from the East End as it were to the West End. It was a different way of life.

Later on things got really bad. He was evil and cruel. He set me up. He knew what time I was getting back to the flat. Then all of a sudden there would be a knock on the door and it would be a friend of his. The friend would come in, waiting for him. He would be very paranoid as he would be doing crack with Max. There'd be no sign of Max and the friend would get fidgety and go.

Then Max would come in and would ask who had been there. And I would say whoever, he was here waiting for you. And Max would say, what did you do with him, what did you do with him? I'd say "Nothing" and then he would start, "I don't trust you. You're a liar, you're a liar. Get in the other fucking room". Then he would pin me down and fuck me to see whether I had just fucked his mate.

On one occasion he took me to a place, a garage in fact, which was a crack-house in Brixton. The guy actually lived in the garage. It was just a garage, quite unfurnished. And there were pipes, tinfoil, coke tins and water bottles everywhere. There would be a few people sitting there. They would be completely on another planet. These were dangerous people, the sort that throw acid in your face. They were nutty, nutty people. And he actually left me in the crack house. He left me there on purpose. And the guy who ran the garage raped me. Max set that up and I knew he had set that up.

I don't know if there was any money in it for Max. Maybe he owed the dealer and paid off a debt using me. He had no sense of morality because he was so fucked up. That's what crack cocaine does to you. I don't know what they are looking for. Some ultimate high, I suppose. But I know that bastard set me up that day and he knows I know it.

He came back an hour later. Where did he go? Why didn't he take me with him?

So there was me being pregnant by a man I now knew to be a perverse, violent bastard. He said that I should get an abortion. I let it float for a bit. He went back to his wife and I went back to my mum's. He would ring me now and then and every time I heard his voice I thought I loved him again. I just don't know why. To this day I just don't know why.

Then there was a phone call. He wanted to meet me. He asked if I was still pregnant. I was only about eight weeks into it. We met up in London and talked about it. We said that an abortion was the best way. I spent the night at his place.

In the taxi the next day on the way to the consultation he was in the front and I was in the back. And I remember looking out of the window and saying to myself, I need to get rid of this child so that I can get rid of the bastard in front of me. And he more or less said the same words to me. And he warned me: if you keep this child I will be in your life forever. He knew he was a mother-fucker. He knew he was a bad man. I'd been attracted to him but the excitement was over, over.

I walked into the clinic feeling confident and had my consultation. Then I had my scan and went back into the room. He was outside. I'll never forget the nurse looking at me and saying: "You have twins. Does that make any difference to your decision?" I knew at that precise moment that it did but I didn't know what the decision would be. I said to her: "Oh my god, I need to think about this. Can I go?" I remember picking up my bag very quickly. I remember running up the stairs, running out on to the street. He was there at the lamppost. I was crying. He said "What are you crying for? What's wrong?" I said, "I'm sorry, I can't do this". He looked at me. "Why? Why?" I said, "Because I've got twins." My nan always used to say to me twins are a blessing. And I just knew I couldn't do it. I knew that that man was going to ruin my life, but I would not, could not get rid of those twins.

I went back to my mum and carried on with the pregnancy. I did see him a bit towards the end of the pregnancy. He tried to get involved a bit more.

By irony, his wife was also pregnant at that time with only a few weeks between us. He was spending a lot of time with her and then towards the end he was flitting between her and me. But the relationship between him and me was completely over. Yet his words still rang true. I'm going to be part of your life for the rest of your fucking life.

Max was a bully and a bastard. His main occupation was robbing. He was known as the Robber and was quite well known. In our time together I was the breadwinner. We moved around a lot to different locations. The flats were always rented. He was an argumentative guy who fell out with people quickly. He would argue with landlords so I found myself moving on very soon. Sometimes he would try to intimidate the landlord. That is what he was like. When we moved on it was always down to my expense: deposits, rent, I was always responsible for everything. He never paid a bloody penny towards anything.

As for his crack-cocaine habit, I supported that. Stupidly I supported that for as long as I was willing. Even after the twin boys were born he thought he had this hold on my life. By that time, I was so emotionally damaged it didn't seem to matter that he came round. In a stupid way I suppose I held on to the hope that he was going to be a good dad. But there were times, I remember, when I was drawing my income support and he would make me drive from Essex to south London to get his crack on the Monday instead of buying my babies' food and nappies. And then he would go out and steal stuff for the babies.

When I had decided not to abort the twins I went back to live with my mother. During my pregnancy it became clear that Max and I detested each other so it was easy to let go. I went to hospital and had the twins.

It was a rough, very complicated pregnancy. When they were delivered one was natural and the other was caesarean. Max was there as he promised he would be, but by then I didn't feel any love for him. In fact I hated him just as much as I loved them. I took the twins back to live with my mum. She said you can come back here as long as you get rid of that man. The love of my family finally got rid of Max.

I was in a vicious circle then and it wasn't until years later that I realised that I was not beholden to this man. It took a lot, a hell of a lot for me to piss him out of my life. He had intimidated me and beaten me and abused me physically and emotionally and I had got used to it, but finally I took him off my phone and I tore up his photos. I just wanted him out of my life completely. I managed it, I succeeded. He's in prison now.

To this day I don't understand why I could have loved and stayed with a man who beat me up and set me up to be used by his mates and a crack dealer.

I can only say that it must have been my demons and the insecurities in me that were so deep rooted. All I know is it will never happen to me again.

Girlfriends in the business

Basically I'm very heterosexual. I started with boys at school and wasn't at all interested in girls and that's been the pattern all my life. All my relationships have been with men. I'm certainly not a lesbian. But I did once have a little encounter with Sonia who always been a very close friend of mine and always will be. She was a working girl too and that's how I got to know her, working in the same sauna.

We were really close, sister close. I don't know how it happened or why it happened. I think we were drunk. We got into bed one night and she started touching me. I never pushed her away. To me it was new experience but it felt nice and it just sort of happened. She was playing with me and went down on me and I remember thinking it felt very nice. It felt different from a man even though she was doing exactly the same things. And because it felt nice I did it back to her and it felt right. It didn't feel disgusting. It did nothing to our relationship, nothing at all. In fact we've joked about it many times. If our partners knew about that, it would be a man's dream. We've never done it again. I'm not saying I would never do it again but I really am too hetero.

She has been my closest friend all my working life. She is incredibly loyal and she is the one person who really knows me more than anyone else in the world. She has typical Yorkshire roots; good values, family values. She's an auntie to my children. She's part of me, part of my family. She's stopped being a working girl now but this means she understands what the business is like and how difficult and stressful it is for me to juggle my home life as a mother with my life as a working girl and as boss of a sauna. In particular she knows the importance of keeping the two lives apart so that my children don't know about my other life. She has children too and a partner who isn't their dad. She's been through it all herself and that is a bond which makes us so close. She's my soul-mate and I trust her absolutely, absolutely.

My friend is also definitely hetero so getting into bed with her that time must have been a flash in the pan for us both. Even so I have been in situations where I find that I do attract lesbian women. I don't mean butch women. I've been approached by really good-looking girls in public places, not in saunas. It puzzles me because I don't think I look like a lesbian at all. I often wonder what there is in me that attracts them. Sometimes when I

57

look at them I find myself thinking, yes, I could do it with them. But I do know that when a woman has made an advance, I have picked up on it quickly and then I have always dropped it.

In saunas when a client wants you do things with another girl, for me and most of us it is a scene, an act. It's not real but it's made to look real. It's what you are there for. You are there to entertain, aren't you? I think that most guys know that it's an act but they don't mind if it's a good one. It's best if the two girls know each other because they have a rapport and can bounce things off one another. If the client wants to see a show, he gets one if he is prepared to pay for it. If he makes a big offer, he wants to see action. That doesn't mean to say you are enjoying it. Two girls can go into the room and act. We are the greatest actresses on the earth.

Sophia

One of my best friends is a French working girl who I look on as a trusted confidante. She is someone who can look after the business short term when I'm on holiday which doesn't happen much or even long term if I was sick. She wouldn't rip you off, she wouldn't steal from you. She'd make sure the place was run right. She cleans and tidies without being asked. She's classy and immaculately dressed and always has been. She's older than the rest of us. She's been sensible and clever over the years and she bought her council place when the money was there. She's steered clear of bad influences by which I mean drugs, smoking and alcohol but she's not judgemental about the girls who do these things. You can do them in front of her and she doesn't have a problem with that. She's obviously always had the courage to say no to them herself. She's bubbly and most other girls like her instantly. I'd call her old school and she has more regulars than most. She is wealthy and she is wise.

I look on her as a real friend. I've been on a few holidays with her over the years. She knows a lot about me, more than most. She adores my children. She always says I am like her sister. One day we were on holiday together in France sharing some wine in the hotel room and she said to me "I look at you like my sister. I love you like my sister". I'll never forget that and I believe it. Even to this day she looks after me and she looks after the shop.

If I were to retire she would be able to take over the shop but I'm not sure she would want to. She sees how much responsibility goes with it. Ten or even five years ago she would probably have said yes but now she sees the struggles I have had and the changing face of the business. In fact she is one of the people who is encouraging me to close the shop because of the pressure on me. We both know deep down it's time to hang up our fishnets.

Friends from the other side of the fence.

Working girls have two completely separate lives. There is a fence between them and you know that people on the other side of the fence look down on us for what we do and what we are. I've been a working girl for the past 20 years and my friends tend to be from that circle. In practice, you alienate yourself a bit from other people because you don't feel normal. You live a completely different lifestyle which is extremely difficult to cover up. So I would say that most of us don't have normal, non-working girl friends unless the normal friends know what we are doing.

It has always baffled me when girls have said that their guys do not know what they are doing. Straight away you know that's a lie. The guys do know. They have to know unless they are completely stupid. They know that their girlfriend is leaving at eleven in the morning with a hold-all with stockings and God-knows-what in it and she doesn't come home until midnight. And those girls will tell you that their guys do not know what they are doing!

Because it is so hard to hide your job, your friends tend to be your work associates. Also it's difficult to get away from this life. It's like a drug. It is a drug, for all who go there — the clients and the girls who work there. I've seen guys who come into a place when they are in their twenties and then in their forties and they are still coming.

So working girls may go on holiday with other working girls. I go on holiday with my children but if they weren't there it would be with another working girl. That's what normally happens.

Chapter 7
FAMILY AND BRINGING UP THE KIDS

Keeping mum about my work

Unless a working girl has done really well and had it off big time, most of us live in council houses. If you are single and have kids the neighbours think you should be living off social security so you have to be careful about what sort of car you drive, the clothes you wear and what you have in the house. Working girls tend to be very frivolous. You earn five hundred quid and you want to blow it. If you go off and shop and come back laden with John Lewis and M&S bags it is difficult to walk up the path and for neighbours to think you are living off social security.

I've been guilty of that in the past and it creates a stir. It makes people talk and it would make me talk. Other people work hard but they can't afford to have a new leather sofa. How come you can do it? You are single, you've got three kids. You have to be careful or you will trip yourself up. People gossip and it only takes one person who knows something or even half-knows something.

When I moved around I found that out, so I learned very quickly to cover up. I took on a part-time job. I went back to nursing part-time for two reasons. One was for tax. The other was because I was going to make sure that no neighbour where I live now was going to think of anything about me and of my kids. My kids have to grow up.

Kids can be cruel too. They hear things that their parents say, they pick it up and things can grow nasty. I used to leave my house with my nurse's uniform on in the morning and make sure my neighbours saw the uniform. I'd get out of sight and I would take it off. Just the same coming home. Before I pulled into my turning I'd find my safe place, I'd put my folder under my arm and I'd have my uniform on when I got out of that car. I still do it now and again though life is different for me now as my children have left home so I don't feel I need to hide so much.

61

Getting my figure back

When I was carrying the twins I put on weight as you'd expect and my bump was big. I was worried that I would lose my figure for good. I didn't feel I could go back to nursing and being a working girl was all I knew. To lose my figure would be the end of my career. But I was blessed with a good genetic and my childhood training as a gymnast meant that my body was slim. I was told I would keep that body for the rest of my life and it was true. The intense training I did when I was a kid means that my body is still strong. The weight I put on having children soon dropped off. I did some exercises but really I put my figure, which still gets attention, down to good genetics and being a busy working mum. Every new client who walks into the shop will look at your body and wants to find a good one if he is going to pay good money. That helps to keep you looking good.

Going back to the business

I took six weeks off for the twins. Going back to work was hard, really hard. I was older, I hadn't any money and nowhere of my own to live. I split the time between my mum and Max's mum. I felt screwed up and fucked. I went back to work quickly because I needed money. And it was shit. I had gone from being someone who had just about everything before my children and now I had nothing. I felt I was having to claw myself up again.

I hated going to work. I kept feeling I should be at home playing with my babies. I kept thinking I would have been quite happy never to have walked into this job. I should have been a nurse, got married, had a few kids. I feel I was made to be a good mother but now I was the victim of circumstance and the dream wasn't to be. The babies were being pushed around and being looked after by different people, mainly my mum.

There was a wonderful woman who I came to know in south London. I called her Auntie Julia. She knew Max's mum. They had both been clippers in the West End, that is girls who worked in clip joints where men would go in expecting to find a working girl but instead were charged stupid sums of money for drinks and mostly never got the girls in the end.

I have never been a clipper. It was a completely different game to working in saunas. Clippers were a scam. Skanking you can call it. Those were the days when Soho was very free and easy but since it tightened up you don't find them around. The clip joints have closed and it isn't easy these days to walk around the West End to find a girl or even a clipper.

I got to know Auntie Julia sitting in a park in Camberwell with my twins. She used to walk through the park and of course the twins were a bit of an attraction. Auntie Julia became my saviour when Max threatened to kill me. I stayed with her and she looked after me for weeks. She would look after my twins when I went to work. She knew what I was doing and that was good. She was protecting me from Max who didn't know where I was staying.

Max often threatened to kill me. He was an evil man. He was always on crack cocaine and that's the worst drug there is. Those rocks are known as the devil's teeth and that's what they are. When I was still with him and would walk in the door with money it was a choice. What are you going to do? Give him the money or take another beating? He was a violent man. He wasn't even a clever man. I've known of men who have beaten friends of mine but they are crafty. They beat them where other people don't see it. Max was just a bastard. He would beat my face. He didn't give a shit if he gave me a black eye. One day he put a hairline fracture in my skull in the street by swinging a four-pack of beer in a carrier bag and I was in hospital in London with the fracture. He swung it and hit the back of my head. I left hospital because there is nothing that could be done and the fracture did heal up.

School runs and school events

Many working girls have kids. In fact bosses prefer them to have kids because they are more dependable. Single working girls can shoot off at any time, but the need to bring up a family is very stabilising. It also seems often to be the case that the male partners of working girls are even less reliable than most men. Some are prone to violence and I've known plenty of working girls whose men, like Max, abuse and beat them. As a result working girls are often single-mums. Part of the difficulty is that men don't want to marry working girls unless they give up the business and though most girls say they would like to quit working, that's pretty much the same for people in other jobs. A successful working girl who has got used to earning £60 to £100 an hour and maybe £300 to £500 a week gets used to having that kind of money. Of course top escort girls such as Brook Magnanti, who was the writer Belle de Jour, could earn £300 in an hour or two, but they are probably less than five percent of all working girls.

Working girl mums have a much more complicated life than ordinary mums. To begin with all of us have the permanent need to conceal from our kids and from neighbours that we are working girls. There is still huge prejudice against the service we provide and we are all terrified at the thought of our kids, when they go to school, being told that your mum is a tart, a slag, a prostitute. We have to organise two completely separate lives. Ordinary mums with help from employers and lots of supportive legislation can get their working hours tailored to fit in with the school run. Some big organisations have flexi-time. There is nothing like that for working girls. A shift is a shift. A few saunas have an appointment system but mostly they don't and girls need to be available when clients come. The starting time usually is 11.00 which is fine for dropping kids at school but finishing time may be 11.00 pm which rules out parent-teacher meetings, school plays and the like.

In many saunas the girls work just two days a week so this reduces the occasions when the mum cannot be present at school functions. For those days child minders have to be found and they cannot be told the real profession of working girls. Describing a sauna as a beauty parlour is a common trick.

Mobile phones help working girls to conceal what we are doing but now that 12 year-olds and upwards all have mobiles they expect to be able to ring mum at any time asking her to sort out problems there and then. This is difficult when a client is waiting on a massage table wanting urgent physical pleasure. When you are a working girl you always feel different from other mums but in bringing up children you have to conform as much as possible to what ordinary society and your children expect from you.

Working girls may be on a shift to 11.00 and not get home until midnight, but the school run at 8.00 onwards is there just as relentlessly. You don't interact with other parents at the school gate either. You don't want other mums and dads to start discussing what work you do. If you are single and childless when you choose to become a working girl your decision is made on one thing only: money. Boiled down to its simplest this means how much money can be made in as little time as possible. When you are a working girl with children, life becomes much more complicated. Part of the complication is the need to protect your children from gossip. This is why quite a number of sauna girls live somewhere that takes an hour or more to get to the shop so that their secret life is safeguarded.

Personally I do my utmost to get to parents' evenings and other school events. This is because I love my kids and want to see them given the best chance in life. In addition I live with the permanent need to safeguard them from rumours and gossip which, if my work was known, would be desperately painful for them. Being an ordinary single mum is not easy. Being a working girl mum is twice as hard.

Holidays and how I cope

School holidays can be a difficult, stressful time for working girl mums. Because we work in shifts, typically two shifts a week, we are clear for all the other days. These are days which I can spend quality time with my kids. We can go to the local pool, go horse-riding or see the latest Harry Potter film. Even so, things aren't that easy. The idea of taking extra time off has always appealed to me and probably to other working girl mums with young kids but through the holidays you need that extra money to do things with the kids. You try and juggle with your friends and your mum and your babysitters. It can be difficult. Sometimes I've put the older one in charge of the younger ones but if you go out and do a typical 12-hour shift when you come home you can walk into all sorts of mayhem. Also, every minute you are away is a constant worry. Your workplace may be miles from home but you still get phone calls from the kids, "mum, mum, mum" every five minutes. It's a stressful time.

On the financial side you have to find extra baby-sitting. For a friend or a baby-sitter you are paying £40 a day. That's OK if the shop is busy and you get 3-5 clients a day but on bad days with few or no clients the baby-sitter cost is harder. I have always found that I am skint most of the holidays. Then you find that you feel guilty for the time you've been away so you tend to compensate, for example taking the children out somewhere and spending the money you've earned, so it's a sort of vicious circle.

In general, school holidays are a stressful time for a working girl mum. If someone rings while I am in the massage room doing a client I don't take the call. In fact I leave my mobile in the girls' back room. I know some girls take it in with them to the massage room but personally I don't. Obviously I have one ear cocked. I know the ring tone of my mobile and straight away I think it must be something to do with home. I never know if it is something serious or just chatty, so when I'm out of the room I ring back missed calls. More often than not when I ring back something has gone on. It is difficult. Many a time I have spent an hour and a half getting to the shop and two hours later something has gone on and I have to drive back home.

My children think I'm a nurse working for a regular company. This may make them think I can't come rushing back whenever they call me but I don't find it easy to invent reasons and if I think I've got to go, I just go.

There are some jobs these days where the companies let you take your kids with you. A few times my kids have asked me: "Mum, can I come to work with you today?" It's a normal question for a kid but for me that is always a throat-choking question. I think that for other forms of work it may be normal for kids to go to work with mum or dad, but for me it doesn't arise. Maybe it raises a bit of suspicion in my kids' minds. This is more noticeable in holidays when you are not there. In term time they come in from school, throw their bags down and then go off for an hour or two with their friends. In holidays it's their mum they want. When I walk in the door at ten o'clock at night I always feel guilty. The only way they've been able to contact me is by my mobile. They don't know my place of work. I get scared. If a policeman called and asked "where's mummy, where does she work?", they wouldn't know. It's something I have to deal with. It's quite heavy.

I think some working girls are a bit more open with their kids about what they do. Personally, I'll take my secret to the grave. People can say to my kids a hundred times over what their mother is or was but they will never hear it from me. I will never admit it to them.

Some working girls I know have involved their daughters in the business, which I envy a bit because it makes their lives easier. I don't mean when they are under age but when they are 17 or 18 they may let them do the receptionist side of things. They take the line if their daughter knows about it why shouldn't she go and get £50 a day being the receptionist. That makes me cringe. I've always wanted to protect my children. If a daughter of mine wanted to go out and become a working girl herself, that would be up to her. Personally I wouldn't want to get her involved for all the money in the world.

66

Chapter 8
GOOD CLIENTS, BAD CLIENTS

Laurence, one of my best clients

Some clients you meet stick in your mind forever. Some you forget the minute they walk out of the door. One of my best was Laurence, known as Lol. He was into racing horses. I think at one time he owned them but he certainly liked backing them and he may have lost everything through gambling. He was a lovely man. Every time he came into the sauna he would bring me a bottle of champagne. There used to be a bookie across the road of this particular sauna and he would shoot over there putting on another hundred quid, another hundred quid. He'd be with us all day.

Lol took a shine to me and one day we had the most fantastic day at the races. We flew to Aintree in his mate's light aircraft and we spent the whole day there drinking Crystal champagne. He spent thousands and he would give me £500 a time telling me to go and put this much on that horse and this much on another. We had a fantastic day and on the way back I had to kick my high heels off. We were running through a field, me in this lovely Chanel suit and waving a champagne bottle above my head. We were late because we were pissed and the pilot was shouting "come on" because it was getting dark.

The pilot, who was a good friend of Lol, landed the aircraft in his own back garden, that is if you can call five acres with a sprawling barn a back garden. What struck me as so funny and still does even to this day is the way his wife and kids came out to greet their daddy as normally as the working classes do when daddy puts his car in the garage. A chauffeur was waiting for Lol and me. Lol dropped me home and as I got out and said my goodbyes he shoved £1,000 in notes in my hand. Smiling as I lay back on the sofa, I was thinking I feel like a million dollars. I'd had one of the best days of my life.

Lol was amazing but sometimes he would disappear and we wouldn't see him for a few weeks. At one point I hadn't seen him for a couple of months. My Baby Ben was seriously ill and I had to take a lot of time off work to be at the hospital. When it was near Christmas Lol suddenly popped in to the sauna when I wasn't there. Another girl who worked there and knew him well, rang me and said Lol came in today. He had been in Germany on business and he had left me £1,000 in an envelope for Christmas, for me and my children. He also gave £1,000 to my friend, the other girl.

We were the ones who worked together a lot at this place. Every time when we were on shift together he would come in. We would all be in the room together for ages and ages, messing around, drinking champagne but if the doorbell went he'd say, "go on, get out. Earn your money. I'll still be here when you get back."

Yes, Lol gave me that fantastic day at the races. My friendship with Lol lasted the whole time I was at that sauna which was a couple of years. I still have the Aintree pass, the little ticket you hang on your lapel to gain entry. I've kept it, and the programme. They remind me of that day.

After Aintree Lol was becoming more and more elusive and a couple of years later we read in the paper what had happened. He had been put in prison for a £2million fraud. So it was "goodbye, Lol", but at least I did get some of the action!

David, the millionaire

I was working for Jimmy at the time when the sauna bell rang and I went to the door. The man who came in was very smartly dressed, short and Jewish, dark hair, immaculate. He had the aura of money about him. He took an instant liking to me, went to the room and I gave him the service he wanted which was simple hand relief. He wasn't a high paying client, not by a long shot, but we got on well. I let him out. He said he would be back and he was smitten with me. I thought I could get him as a good client; very rich.

As I let him out of the door I saw he had parked right outside the sauna. And blow me, he got into a cream Rolls Royce. I was struck dumb that a man could park a Roller with his own number plate outside the sauna.

Anyway, true to his word he did come back. I knew he would. He was flashy and cocky, in his forties, a bit overpowering, a snap-my-fingers-and-everyone-comes-running sort of person. That's what he was and that's probably how he had got what he got. Certainly he was different and I got invited out for a drive in the Rolls Royce. So off I went leaving Vicky the other girl there. She was saying "go on, piss off, go, go, go".

Inside the Rolls Royce was fantastic. We drove round and it became apparent to me that he was a show-off. We drove round to Oxhey and went for an hour or so. He was driving, not a chauffeur. It made me laugh because I thought how typical. Little man, little cock, big car.

He became a regular. I was under no illusions that I was going to get thousands of pounds out of him but in my eyes he was a nice little client. He wasn't my type of person to have an affair with. He was too cocky, too flash. He wouldn't even have been a sugar daddy because he was too mean. He was a typical Jewish man: he had made his money and he kept his money.

But I did get a holiday out of him. After he had been a client for a few months he invited me on a holiday. To his wife it was a business trip at a time when she was skiing. Very likely she was shagging a ski instructor. David had a friend, an American record producer called Marvin who was something else. Nothing like David at all. He asked me to bring a friend too so I chose a really lovely working girl I knew. In those days it was easy. We didn't have kids. An all-expenses-paid holiday in the sun was too good to pass up. I had worked with Jade in Madam X's place. She was pretty with long blonde hair and was nice enough though a bit moody. She was free at the time. "Oh yeah, I'll come with you ".

It was to be a luxury holiday in Tenerife and his brother lived there. We didn't get paid and we knew they would screw us whenever they felt like it but that was fine so off we went. But things didn't work out quite as expected. I am very laid back and just wanted to lie on the beach but then I found that being around David in different circumstances I couldn't stand him. I didn't like the way he strutted. I didn't like the way he spoke to the receptionist at the hotel.

When we were booking into the hotel there was some sort of problem. The hotel itself was beautiful and I don't think that whatever it was could be serious but because he wasn't getting attention he banged the desk with his hand. My back went up and I thought "you pig". The woman came over to him and he said "Do you know who I am and what I own in London? If my

69

staff were like you they'd be sacked". That's how we started the holiday and I was thinking, oh my God, I've got stuck with seven days of you. Things got sorted out with the hotel but he had given me the hump.

We went to the room and unpacked. All his suits and shirts were immaculate. We had a phone in the room. "You can make an outside call, but don't ever answer that phone".

It was his whole attitude with everything that I hated. I saw the snobbery in him. When we went to dinner he would snap his fingers in the air to get the waiters to come. It was awful.

He thought he was God's gift and I secretly laughed to myself because in the bedroom I once caught him adjusting his hair-piece but he didn't see me. He also irritated me by strutting about whistling. This guy needed loosening up and I was about do to just that.

One night we had been there for a couple of days. I said to Jade, he's pissing me off. He's rude, he's arrogant and I'm going to fuck him up tonight. So she and I decided to be naughty. The men went down to the dinner leaving us behind getting ready. We did it on purpose and we did ourselves up to the nines. I put on the shortest skirt and the highest heels and I walked all the way through that restaurant. It was a top class restaurant where you dressed for dinner. But Jade and I didn't dress for dinner that night, we undressed for dinner. David's face was a picture when we walked through. Marvin's expression was "go on girls" but David's hit the floor. I sat down next to David with the whole restaurant watching, in their pearls. He looked at me and said "Are you on a wind-up"? And I said "I'm going out after dinner." He said "Are you" and I said "yes", and that is exactly what I did.

We had dinner in silence. As soon as we had finished I got up, picked my bag up and said, "Come on, Jade" and we fucked off to another hotel over the road where there was a big disco. We stayed out all night for deliberate badness. I rolled back into the room looking like shit. I walked into the pool area. Everyone knew we were with them and everyone knew we went off for the night. That's what I wanted. I wanted to piss him off.

After that he calmed down with me and we calmed down with each other. We knew where each other was coming from. I told him, "Listen, I maybe ain't got the money you've got, but I ain't fucking rude. You are a very rude man and all your money ain't got you no manners".

After that holiday it was quite clear I didn't want to see him and he didn't want to see me. He did ring me to make sure I was OK. I said "thank you very much, David. It was nice to meet Marvin" and that was it.

Inspector Gadget

One day the shop bell rang. My shift was with Maureen, a slim blonde girl with a nice figure and beautiful legs. We clicked on the CCTV and saw a man we didn't recognise. He could have been to the shop before and seen another girl but equally he could be a new client. We went to the door together, unlocked it and in he came. If a sauna has several girls working at once a client usually gets a choice unless the system is to put the girls forward in rotation. This man seemed a bit nervous as he looked at the two of us. Then with a smile he touched my arm to show that I was the one he had picked. Maureen went back to the parlour where we answer the telephone, watch TV, drink endless cups of tea and wait for the next client.

I took him into my preferred room, asked him if he would like a cuppa and what his name was. He probably said John. I'm not sure now because it didn't matter and we assume clients invent their names. So far nothing out of the ordinary. This John was clearly educated and well spoken. I asked if he wanted a shower and he said he'd had one that morning. When he got undressed he smelled nice so I knew he was telling the truth.

He was down to his pants when I brought the tea in. I guessed he was about fifty-five. A slim body, about 6' tall, brown hair with some grey at the temples, and only a little body hair on his chest. He asked about the cost of my services and chose the basic massage and hand relief. I massaged him for about ten minutes and he hardened up nicely. For about two minutes I worked his cock, he came and I wiped him up. He said he'd have shower at home, dressed and I took him to the door. All this was quite routine and ordinary. What was a bit different was that before he left he put his arms lightly round me and kissed me on the lips in a way which wasn't passionate but seemed as though he meant it. The way he thanked me also seemed gentle, courteous and sincere. He asked whether I worked here every day and I told him my usual shifts. None of this was out of the ordinary and I didn't think too much about it.

71

A week later he rang the shop and asked to speak to me. His voice was distinctive and I immediately could recall his face. He came in punctually an hour later and everything looked set to continue as before. He gave me two £20 notes and undressed. I began to massage his back and as I did so his face was to one side looking at me. Hesitantly he asked if he was allowed to see my breasts. I almost said, "yes, but it will cost another £10, or £20 for a full strip" but something made me hold back. It was my usual hope that this would enable him to come quicker but something different went through my mind. Was I being set up? Could this be someone from the Revenue or the council sent to spy on me and the sauna? Could it be a plain-clothes cop? I decided to risk it. Clothes off isn't a crime and if John was some official or other he would be digging his own grave if he wanted me to go further. Off came my bra.

He came to see me once a week or so for the next few weeks and I liked him. He was definitely top drawer but not in a snobbish way. On the massage table he told me a bit about himself. He was divorced, had grown-up children and lived quite close. He'd seen an advertisement in the paper and had wanted to see what happened in a sauna. He had tried another local one but thought that ours sounded better. As I start by mistrusting everything I am told by clients I didn't take much notice but I did feel that he was genuine in what he said and could become a regular client of mine. That was worth going for.

The next time he came to see me the bra came off and so did my panties. John told me that he got turned on by black stockings — all men do and I wear them all the time in the shop — but then he added that he liked wearing them too. He assured me he was totally hetero but the sensation of sheer hold-ups added to his enjoyment. I told him that he was just getting in touch with his feminine side and he liked that. Sure enough, when he came to the sauna a week later he was wearing black hold-ups underneath his jeans and he had brought me a lovely pair of open-crotch panties from Ann Summers. He enjoyed watching me put them on.

From then on for the next few times he came he would bring me something to wear: panties, a bra with open tips for the nipples, fishnet hold-ups or a lacy thong. Sometimes he would wear the same thing he was giving me. All this added to his fun and was no trouble to me.

John was becoming more adventurous in what he asked of me. Massaging

72

his cock with my breasts was one of his favourites. I should have upped the price but he was coming in so regularly every week when the shop was much too quiet so I just stuck with the two £20 notes that he would leave beside the massage table.

The next development was that he would bring different forms of flavoured gels from Ann Summers which are used to provide an added tingle and taste when used on his body or mine. These were accompanied by a vibrator and a set of plastic beads with which he used to rub my clit.

After John had been a few times with these things I told him I would call him Inspector Gadget: Inspector because initially I had thought he might be an inspector; and Gadget because of the different things he brought to have fun with. One of them was a little flogger made of soft leather. He asked if he could whip my pussy. I'm absolutely not into pain but I said he could do it providing it was very light and if I said "too hard" or "stop" he would do so. I had to trust him. It was a leap of faith but it was fine. The sensation was quite fun and certainly wasn't painful. Stimulating rather. He liked me to do the same thing to him though he wanted me to whip him a bit harder than he did me. Sometimes his cock would be marked but he told me the marks went away in a day or two.

The next step happened after about two months when very hesitantly he asked if he could go down on me. From puberty onwards and all my life my clit has been the focus of my pleasure. I get a wonderful orgasm from my clit whereas having a vibrator or a cock in my fanny doesn't do much for me unless my clit is being worked at the same time. The Rampant Rabbit sold in all the sex shops these days can do the trick but isn't as nice as a man's tongue.

It was an important moment when for the first time he asked me if I would let him lick my pussy. I had no hesitation at all and was glad he had asked. He knelt at the end of the massage table, I spread my legs and in the next five minutes he gave me a wonderful orgasm which left me feeling weak at the knees. After that I had to rush to the loo to pee which I always have to do when I have come. He was obviously pleased that I let him do this which made him feel special. From then on as an absolutely standard part of our session he would lick my pussy and give me an orgasm. He used to tease me, saying that perhaps I should be paying him rather than the other way round.

73

The next stage was reverse oral, often called 69. He would lie on his back and I would get on the massage table facing the other way. It is just big enough and I would adjust my position so that my pussy was at the best angle for his tongue. He often said he wanted me to delay coming but normally he had me off in less than five minutes. I'd work on his cock. If he wore a condom I'd bring him off orally, otherwise I'd put one of his special creams on his cock and use my hands.

When we had both come sometimes he would give me a lovely back massage. He was good at it. I liked feeling his thumbs and fingers digging hard up and down my shoulder blades and around my spine. That could go on for 20 minutes or more but would have to stop if we heard the doorbell meaning another client was coming in. Mostly we have two girls working at any time so I could always hope that the new client would go with the other girl. Even so, I have my regulars and I don't want to lose them by passing them on to another girl.

Once or twice Inspector Gadget would ask if he could shave my pubes. I like to keep a small strip of hair above my pussy and never have it fully bare. I told him that is how I like it and said he could shave me providing he left a strip. He had brought an electric razor and I lay back and spread my legs. By now I felt sure I could trust him to be as good as his word and he was. He did a nice job and the razor left a smooth finish. Clearly he enjoyed doing it and for me anything that keeps a client regular must be good. He did all these things and I was still only charging him £40. The other girls would think I was barmy but by now he was my best regular, coming in twice or even three times a week. In fact he was by far the most frequent regular in the shop. That justified giving him his usual price instead of doubling it for the services he wanted.

Most unusually I developed a real friendship with Inspector Gadget. It was against my personal rules but somehow he was quite different. He regularly told me how much he cared for me and it was obvious that he wanted me to respond. "Lie to me" he would say, and I would reply "I love you too". At first this was just a little ritual for me but later I found that I really meant it. I wasn't in love with him but I did feel deep affection because he was so good to me.

Inspector Gadget is an example of how continuing visits by a regular can enhance the client's pleasure and sometimes even give pleasure to the girl.

74

Both sides know what they like. The girl sets out her boundaries early on because all of us have limits which we won't cross whatever the money. Both sides know what to expect, what the session will consist of, how long it will last and what the price will be. Both sides part feeling satisfied with what has taken place. For the client it is uncomplicated pleasure and in so many ways it seems to be a good solution for men's need for sex. It is only a pity that visiting a working girl often entails some sort of cheating unless the client is genuinely single. Personally I'd much rather a partner of mine cheated by going to a working girl (though I'd be deeply upset if I wasn't good at making him satisfied) rather than having an affair with another woman with emotional strings and ending in tears all round.

Inspector Gadget was one of my best clients. He wasn't the wealthiest by any means but he was generous in different ways. He would remember my birthday and bring me something. He even expected me to remember his birthday so you can see that our professional relationship had developed into a form of friendship. That was unusual for me. My golden rule about not having any relationship with clients was pushed about as far as it would go.

I used to say that he was funny in what he wanted from me. He was very tactile and he said he was a romantic. He regularly kissed my lips which is all I would allow. When he asked for deep French kissing I didn't allow it however many times he tried. He also liked kissing my face which he did very softly all over. I don't like having this done. I can't explain why but I think most working girls are the same. It seems too intimate — the sort of things our partners would do, though generally they don't. I let Inspector Gadget do it because I became really fond of him. I realised that I was breaking my own rule but it didn't seem to matter. His regular £40 twice or three times a week made up for it. On a few occasions when I was skint and had a bill to pay he would hand me £200 representing five sessions paid for in advance.

I still see Inspector Gadget. He's often told me that I am the only working girl he wants to come to but now he knows that I am planning to quit the business I suppose he may be looking elsewhere. In my shop the other girls would be glad to take him on when I leave. One thing is sure: I'll never forget him. He may become the last link to my life as a working girl. He became a friend. He treated me with respect like an ordinary woman, not like a working girl, and wanted to give me pleasure before he took his own.

He never failed me even when I let him down. He was always on the other end of the phone for me. He never once lost his temper with me. He was extremely patient and caring.

Bad clients

Good clients are the ones who come to see me regularly, pay well and are polite. In theory the client expects a certain amount of time that he is paying for. A difficult client is one who wants a lot of attention and maybe pesters to have sex without a condom, which he doesn't get. Also he may have haggled about the price. When he has come he knows that's it and he has a shower if he wants to and clears off. You want him to come back so you spend a little time with him to make him feel good. If there is another client waiting you have to juggle the timing a bit but it makes clients realise you are in demand, which is good.

Bad clients are the ones who hurt you physically. It doesn't happen much in saunas which is why they are safer places to work. Men can be rough when they are having sex. You get used to that because it comes with the job but you don't look forward to having those clients back.

Some clients smell. We tell them that they must shower before we get going and usually they do that OK. They may want to kiss you. Girls have their own way of dealing with that. Most don't mind a peck on the lips but many draw the line at deep tongue or French kissing. This may be because of their worries about catching things such as cold-sores or worse, or it may be that they think that deep kissing really belongs to their boyfriends or partners.

A very few clients get out of hand and it is hard to control them, particularly if they are pissed when they come. You can't afford to turn a client away just because he has come straight out of the pub but it's not nice. One client left some love bites round my neck and really hurt me. I pushed him off me and told him to scram. When my partner saw them he got really angry because he thought they were real love bites. Some girls' partners accept that their girl gets fucked every working day because he wants her to earn a living and, if he's a real ponce, to support him as well. But they get jealous and vicious if they think that their girl is having an affair with another man. When the client came back and I told him to get lost. I wouldn't have him again for twice the money.

76

Having a pissed client is always a gamble. He may be too pissed to have sex and then just go to sleep in a chair. He may get nasty and violent but that's rare. In Germany the girls have alarm buttons to press so that a heavy can come in and throw the client out. That's unusual here. Pissed clients sometimes throw-up and that's awful. There's nothing to do but clean up after him. Once the client is in the room with you he's your responsibility. If he's pissed the vital thing is to get the money off him first and never look a drunk in the eye.

The worst clients are the ones who are verbal and abusive. They think that because they have paid for half an hour of your time they can treat you like shit. Bad language and pawing you all over like a piece of meat. You feel like shit at the end of it. Telling the other girls about it is a form of self help. And we laugh as much as we can. Laughter is very much a self-defence mechanism in the sauna when clients make you feel like the lowest thing on earth.

Clients who get 'rolled' by sauna girls

Sometimes sauna girls get their own back on clients by 'rolling them'. For example, in Madam X's sauna the guys who came in had plenty of money. One client had had a big win on the horses. He was inoffensive but very very drunk. He comes in; it's ten o'clock at night. He's pissed up. He gets into the Jacuzzi. It's a hot steamy room and all his clothes are on the floor with money everywhere. He hasn't a clue what he's got and what he hasn't and he goes to sleep in the Jacuzzi. That would be the moment when a girl would dip his money. Or it could be her boyfriend sitting there who would do it so as not to get her in trouble. The money might be in the guy's pocket or in his wallet. He would be robbed. The boy friend very likely would be her pimp so taking money off a drunk punter would be like taking candy from a kid.

Mind you, you don't see boyfriends in saunas much. If they are pimps they are happy to see their girls earning money but clients don't want to see other men hanging around. What goes on in a sauna should be private. I would never want a boyfriend or partner sitting round in my place. He might come to pick me up or drop something off but that's it. I don't have a ponce and I am a very private girl.

A client who gets rolled would never call the police and we sauna girls are

77

very good at dealing with things. The story would be something like: "you fell asleep; another client walked in here and stole your money. Now get up and get fucking out. How stupid are you, falling asleep! We can't keep an eye on your money."

Dipping the client is another word for the same thing. For example, if the client goes to the toilet or a shower the girl gets into his pockets. I don't think that goes on much now. I've never done it but I've seen it done. In fact one time I saw a client who was pissed and was just setting himself up for being dipped and I warned him so it didn't happen. In my sauna I'd fire any girl who did it. Also we have a bag that hangs on a hook in each massage room so that when the client takes his clothes off he can put his valuables in the bag. If he goes to the shower or the toilet he can take the bag with him.

Chapter 9
SOME REASONS FOR REMEMBERING CLIENTS

On a normal working day I see about three clients. It used to be more but the recession has hit saunas hard. Five clients or more in a shift of eight to ten hours are a good day's work for me these days. If I take three as being average and do three shifts a week, I have seen 450 clients a year. Most of them fade from my memory as soon as the door closes behind them but inevitably some stand out.

Longest regulars

I have a handful of guys who I have seen at my sauna for as long as I've been in this place, which is over 10 years. I can almost set my clock by them. I know when they are coming in. They have my personal mobile number because I have known them that long. They are not interested in seeing anybody else and if they come to the door they will go away if I'm not there. Nine out of ten know when I am there or when I should be there and usually they ring me first.

Normally it is not a good idea to give clients your phone number. It becomes embarrassing if they text you something out of the ordinary. When you are at home you don't want to hear from clients on your days off. It's only happened to me a few times and the clients I give my number to don't do that. On occasions when I have given out my number thinking that I knew the client OK it has gone wrong. It can be intrusive particularly if they text me things that are dirty. If it's something short like "Will u be there 2day?" that's fine.

My ten-year long clients vary a bit about coming in. I suppose you could say about twice a month is normal. Every week I am there I see at least one or two of them. If everything else fails, I have that to rely on. I never ring them even if the shop is very quiet and I need the business though I have known girls who do that. I only ring them if I have just missed their call. Then I ring them back straight away. Otherwise I never call a client, ever.

Over ten years they always want the same service so I know what they expect and what I can give them. Basically they just want standard service: fucking, oral or hand relief. That's how I like it. Just normal service.

Even though they have been coming for ten years I don't have any real friendship with them. In the room I don't ask them about their families and they don't ask about mine. It's just about what is happening in the room, the weather, what you are doing at the weekend and what you are having to eat.

Most generous

Inevitably the clients who stick most in my mind are the ones who are most generous. I've described Lol in another chapter. Lennie was a little old man who bought me a car, a red BMW 325. This was in 1997. He paid about six grand for it. It was four years old. That was a very generous present and I don't know if he had redundancy money or if he had gone off his head. First he was quite sweet on another girl. Maybe she took too much money out of him but it went pear-shaped. She was a bit unreliable anyway so he catches on to me. He kept on being a bit over-generous and I just thought he's an old guy going off his head. He would come in every time I was there and kept saying he would help me. He didn't have much of a service but he always paid me an extra £30 on top.

I was talking to him one time. Actually I was earning loads of money and I was using taxis to and from home for £30 each way. He used to say to me, all that money you are spending in taxis! He would offer to give me a lift home and obviously I would say no because I don't want clients knowing where I live. I don't care who they are. He asked me if I drive, and I said yes and I was saving up to get a car. So he came in one morning. I had not long started my shift, and he says: "I've been thinking. All this money you've been paying out on taxis, and you won't let me take you home…" I used to say, "Lennie, you don't want to be coming out after 11 at night. And I get a lift home most of the time anyway".

So this time, he comes into the shop and says "I've got a present for you. Get dressed. You've got to come out with me."

I say: "What is is?"

"It's a surprise, a surprise."

We are walking round the corner and he puts something in my hand. I say; "What's that?" and he says "Don't look at it."

But I can feel that it is a key. We turn past the corner and there is a red BMW 325 series; and it is mine.

Then I had to go with him to the garage to change the ownership and do all the paperwork because he didn't know my real name. It must have seemed funny to the salesman in the showroom to have a guy buying me a car and he didn't know my name.

Afterwards he just carried on being my client. I was a bit funny at first because I was thinking: God, what do I have to do to pay back this car?" But it wasn't like that. He just carried on like before. The strange thing is that after a few months I didn't hear from Lennie anymore. I don't know what happened to him. Maybe he died. I never went to his house so I don't know where he lived. He might have remembered my address from when I took ownership of the BMW. But he just disappeared. Perhaps he went to a nursing home or went off his head a bit. Still, I had this beautiful BMW which I kept for a couple of years. Then I traded it in when I upgraded to a brand new convertible which I drove straight out of the show room. I remember lighting a fag and pressing the button which opened the roof. I had the biggest smile ever on my face.

The car was the biggest thing I have ever had from a client. I have had clients help me out with cash when I've been in a jam. I've had client who I gave a minimum service and still gave me a couple of hundred quid. I had another guy who said to me, I don't care what it is you want, if you need £500 or a grand and you need it desperately, ring me. I did that once and he was there the next day and he gave me a grand. It was a gift, not a loan. That was about two or three years ago, when the good times for the sauna business were dropping off but there were still some rich clients about. I don't think any of my clients now would be as ready with money like that.

Fattest

Fat clients are memorable for the wrong reasons. I remember one client called Bob. The doorbell goes and I look through the spy-hole as usual.

You can only see the upper half in a distorted way. I open the door and the guy is massive. 30 stone I'd say. He comes in sideways. I was with Lizzie. We both stand back not wanting to do Bob but it was my turn. She had done him before and knew him. In fact he was a regular at the time. Once a month.

I take him into the room and literally I have to lift up rolls and rolls of fat to find what I am looking for. It is a tiny, tiny willy, two inches maybe. Guys who are that fat know they can't have sex so they just want hand relief unless you are brave enough to go down there to give them oral. Trouble is the condom comes off in your mouth.

One day Bob simply broke the massage table and we had to get a new one. He kept coming to see us. We didn't charge him for a new massage table.

Biggest dicks and smallest

As soon as a guy drops his trousers I naturally want to see what kind of cock I am dealing with. I am sussing out the work I've got ahead of me. In addition, working girls can classify clients by their appearance and manner. Sometimes we can look at the man and know exactly what he is going to have before he even asks for it. For example we can say "This one's a muff-diver or someone else is only hand-relief". The cheapest clients are just £40 with hand relief. Muff-divers pay better. Muff-diving means licking pussy. It used to be an extra service but now it gets thrown in with everything else. If a guy wants to muff-dive he probably gets 15 minutes of massage first. He's paid for half an hour and you've done 20 minutes which you know in your head without having to look at any clock. You'll let him muff-dive for five minutes when he is coming to the end of the service. If a client says he wants to go down on you and finish up with hand-relief, oral or fucking, that package will be £70 - £80 these days.

Guys with big cocks vary in attitude. Some are modest about it or don't even know that they are big. Others never stop going on about it as though it is the most wonderful thing on earth. I've seen a 10 inch cock fully hard. Cocks that size can hurt the inside of my pussy and I can feel quite tender the next day. Occasionally I couldn't work the next day. Nowadays, if a guy is really huge I might not let him inside me. Some can fuck you without hurting you but you can't be sure that they'll be gentle. I know other girls that refuse really big cocks too.

82

A few men bring toys to put inside me but I don't like it. You can't be sure they are clean. They have to pay me a lot extra. If I've checked the toy out and believe it to be properly clean I would ask him for at least £20 on top of the service that he already wanted. I won't let him put it up my bum, but if he wants it up his bum I do it. I have a few clients who like that. They pay me well, typically £100.

The smelliest

We do have to put up with some really smelly, filthy clients. They are always the ones who say they have just had a shower or a bath, which makes us laugh. Sometimes they have just come straight from work so you know they are lying. Or you get the ones who go in the shower, they come out and their bodies are bone dry. Or they shower and just their top half is wet. They don't understand that they've got to wash their willies. It amazes me that grown men can shower and still smell. It's not always the ones who come in looking scruffy. It can also be the ones who are suited and booted.

Every girl has clients who stink. Some are really bad. You go into the room and you see dirt on their feet. You can smell feet, you can smell cock, you can smell bum, you can smell piss, you can see shit, and some really reek. When they've gone the place reeks and the girls go round splashing air freshener everywhere. If the clients are old we take them to the shower ourselves. We have one client in particular who knows he smells. We take him and wash him very very carefully. But the others are the ones who think they are clean but they stink. It means that you are retching in the room. Some put their arse up in the air when you are massaging them and you think, oh dear!

When you are doing a two-girl the girls are looking at each other in the mirror at the side and pulling faces at each other. The client has his face down but his shitty arse is up in the air so he doesn't see the girls' expressions and that they are holding their noses and making fun. You just have to laugh about it. Even when you leave and get into the fresh air you can still smell it. You can go home with that smell up your nose all night. Your hands stink and no matter how much you wash them they are still smelly. I've had clients like that in all the saunas I've worked in. We always say, poor wives. What they have to put up with. No wonder they don't want sex.

83

Chapter 10
SHIFTS

A typical working shift in a sauna is twelve hours, from eleven to eleven. When saunas were very busy, particularly in the West End, there were split shifts from ten or eleven in the morning to six. Then the next shift would be from six to one in the morning.

Escort agencies are different. Some agencies run 24/7 call-outs. These are different girls. Sauna bosses need their girls to be in the place throughout their shift. One big change is that bosses now allow girls to work in the sauna using their own mobile phones. That used never to be allowed but bosses have had to become more flexible because saunas are a dying business and it is hard to keep them going. The recession has been terrible for saunas. Clients have dried up. If a girl is allowed to use her mobile in the sauna the boss has got to be sure that she is not just fixing an appointment for the client to come to her flat and so avoid paying a fee to the sauna. This is another reason why bosses prefer to hire working girls with families to support. They can't take clients home. Home visiting or "outcalls" is a growing part of the business but the risk is higher and the days of girls being driven to the client are long gone.

The fact that working girls often live an hour or more away from the sauna is another safeguard for the boss. The girl would need to get her cards put up in places near her flat which would be a considerable way from the sauna. Clients aren't going to travel an hour to get there. It's a fluid arrangement these days in which there has to be a bit of trust on both sides. The boss doesn't want girls to take clients from the sauna but in the end all that matters is that she does enough clients in the sauna to pay her way there. If she is doing other clients in her flat, good luck to her.

When girls go on holiday or are ill, the boss needs to get their shifts covered. I've been lucky. I think I'm a good boss because I know what it is like to have worked for bad ones. This means my girls are willing to rally round to get spare shifts covered for me. This is what is keeping my sauna open at a time when the sauna business is going downhill and the recession has made things really bad. But the girls and I all know that the shifts have to be covered. There has to be shift money coming in as well as a payment per client. That's not profit. It's just what keeps the door open.

Right now it's really hard for the girls. The shift money they pay keeps going up to pay rent, council tax, heating and repairs while at the same time the number of clients is going down. Sauna girls are caught in the middle. The days of sauna girls earning several hundred a day are long since gone. Clients are getting more demanding. They want more services for less money and they haggle. The girls have a minimum rate which typically is a body massage finishing with hand relief, which is sometimes called a happy ending. They won't work for less than £40 which will be about 20 minutes or less if they can get away with it.

Other services cost more. In terms of other jobs outside, a theoretical wage of £80 an hour upwards for being a working girl sounds great, but if there are only one or two clients a day and sometimes none, £80 for a 12 hour shift works out at £6.66 an hour before the shift fee and the per-client payments have come off the money she has taken. You are getting close to the national minimum wage.

Shift money payable to the shop varies. In my place it is £50 for the first client and £20 for every other client. If the girl gets no clients she doesn't pay anything and that is awful for her and for the shop. If she gets three clients at £60 each she ends up with £90 to take home. For a 12 hour shift that is £7.50 an hour. Cleaning ladies get £10 an hour these days so the key to being a successful working girl is to get shifts in a place that is busy in its own right and then to treat the clients so well that they become regulars. These days if a girl does five clients in a shift at £60 each she has had a good day and takes home £170 but this is still way off the good years. In the early 'noughties girls would think nothing of going home with £300 for a shift.

The pay of escort girls working for an agency has a different tariff. Brooke Magnanti who was an escort known as Belle de Jour charged her clients £300 of which she paid £100 to the agency so she needed just one client a day to clear £200. The clients would get more time and they could have plenty of variations too. Brooke described on television how some clients liked having her romping around in food or wearing fetish clothes. Also she was willing to do overnight stays costing £800 to £1,300. This is a different part of the market to the sauna. Some of my girls and I have to do a school run first thing in the morning and get back home to do an evening meal.

Brooke Magnanti was single so that made things much easier.

In my sauna I have continued to employ girls in their 30s and 40s. We cater for men who value their experience. Some of our clients have been regulars for ten or even fifteen years and we rely on them. At the end of every day I know how many clients each girl had done so I know how much each girl is earning for the shop in a given week or month. In present circumstances I know that some of my girls are really struggling to pay their own rents and other necessities. I try to bear this in mind all the time and I would hate to have to sack a girl who wasn't doing enough clients to pay her way. But like in any business I've got to keep the bills paid and the door open. Some girls do enough business for the shop but are unreliable. Others are the opposite. In the sauna it is nice to have a bit of both. Reliability is something. Mostly things sort themselves out because girls who don't do enough clients leave of their own accord.

I am lucky. I have had to put my charges to the girls up and up and up, but the girls are still there. I must be doing something right.

Chapter 11
UPS AND DOWNS OF BEING A WORKING GIRL

Good days and bad days

Obviously a good day is when you've earned good money. No hiccups. You like the girl you are working with. You are busy, which means a steady number of clients. You look at the clock and it's five already. Next time you look it's four or five hours later. You've earned your money and you go home.

If some of the clients are new, that's even better. A new client is one you want to turn into a regular. Regulars are what every working girl wants not just because of the money now and in the future but because she knows that she is doing it right. The regular knows what he wants, the working girl knows what he wants and she gives it him. It is a straightforward service that leaves both of them satisfied.

You can say that the bad days are just the exact opposite of the good days, only that there seem to be many more of them now. A bad day is when you get in on time, you sit there feeling all optimistic and nothing happens. Some days when you walk in you get the vibes that it's going to be bad. For me it happens when I'm at home. I feel it's going to be a bad day but I say to myself I must go in. I've got a shift to cover. So I go in but always it turns out that I shouldn't have gone. No money, no clients and the phone's not ringing.

Actually a quiet phone doesn't mean much as such. Sometimes it rings all the time and it pisses you off because you answer it and nobody is coming through the door. You get men who ring off without speaking. You get men who ask you who is working today and what they look like. So we go through the usual descriptions. Typically for myself I say she is a tall leggy brunette in her early forties. Then they ask what the girls will do and we all say the same thing. "Ten pounds for a half-hour massage and if you want anything else you discuss it with the girl".

89

They may ask what is the price for the additional services and we say "it begins a £30". This means the client knows he has got to pay at least £40. Actually that is the bottom price and we are always looking to average at least £60 to £80. But some clients only want a body massage and hand relief. They'll get it for £40 or £50.

On a bad day you get these phone calls and nobody comes. You go home with no money and you are out of pocket when you have paid the petrol money and, if you are a working girl mum, the child minder. That's the soul destroying day. You've got an hour's drive and you've got no money after a shift of nine or even 12 hours. That's a really bad day money-wise and a bad day all round.

Another kind of bad day is when you have a really horrible client. Some of them pay well but they are horrible. For example they can be rough with me and be hurtful.

For me as a boss a bad day is when big bills come in. I know what's in the bank and there isn't enough. Or there's a shower that's not working and I can't afford to fix it. Or there are problems at home which inevitably come first and have a big knock-on effect if not dealt with or resolved.

Another problem that makes for a bad day is when I know that a girl has been "knocking the shop". That means she's not recording some of the clients she sees so she pockets all the money and doesn't make the contribution to all the bills I have to pay as overheads. You have to try to keep on top of that. You try to let them know that you know what they are doing.

There are ways I have of checking how many men they are doing in a day, and if I go in the next day and when I know they have done five or six and have only recorded three I know they are cheating me. I could just say "piss off" and go find another sauna. I don't do that much because there have to be things I turn a blind eye to so long as they are not making me bankrupt.

They are taking the piss if they have five clients in and don't record four of them. I do understand them saying they've done none when I know they've done one. I just don't want to find out about it. I've been in the business plenty long enough. I've done all that myself. I know when they are doing it but I have to turn a blind eye some of the time.

Advertising myself and the shop

Getting clients, like in any business, is the name of the game. The standard way used to be advertising in the local papers, the personal section. In its day this was cracking, absolutely cracking. It was expensive, mind you. More expensive than any other kind of advertisement in them but that's where most of your trade was coming from. But, over the last couple of years we are not allowed to advertise in local papers anymore which has made it difficult for a lot of saunas.

I've been quite lucky because my place has been established for 30 years and we are described as a health and beauty salon but these days to advertise you've got to show a diploma with a beauty qualification. The newspapers would like to take our advertisements because they are losing money but they've got to cover themselves and so they ask to see a diploma. My girls don't have that and even if they did I don't think any of them would want to submit personal details and put themselves on the line.

There was a time when we had problems with the council which was asking for names of two of the people in the shop. You get this in Westminster, for example. You have to submit yourself to the council and take your passport for them to look at before you could work in the borough. We've had a bit of that where I work now. It was something to do with the Revenue and the council wanted two people's names who worked here, but that was some time ago.

Now that press advertising has been stopped we depend more on putting cards into newsagents and other shops. Some will take them, some won't. It's a cheap way of advertising and it does work. If you put enough cards out and keep on top of it you find that people do read the cards. You can't put them in phone booths now but I wouldn't want that anyway. It's for so called "models" who work in flats. Advertising a business is a different ball-game from advertising a flat. The business has to be a bit more discreet. You are registered with the council, you pay your business rates and you are in the public face. You have to be careful about what you flaunt.

The location of the shop is important to attract passing business. We have a sign outside the shop saying "sauna and massage" and people know what it means. Years ago we used to have a free-standing board outside the entrance to the shop. Whoever was in first would put it outside the front door. Quite a few places where I worked had a board saying "Sauna and massage open" but that's a thing of the past.

Apart from cards we use the Internet. I have a website now. I was very reluctant to begin with and I think a lot of bosses were because there was a time when the Revenue went on to the Internet and went down the lists of saunas. Previously they used to do it by going through the newspaper advertisements. I'm rather the old school and I always have in my head that if they want to get you, that is what the Revenue will do.

With the Internet advertising it took me a long time to get my head round it. I just didn't want to be on the Internet and I took a lot of persuading but now all the saunas do it and so do many of the girls who work from their own flats. I have a friend who set up a site for me which seems to have really kicked in and worked. That's OK but I am very careful about what I put on the site. If I put more details in I could probably get more clients but I don't want to do that. I don't want to say what I am actually doing. There's also a well known site called Punternet which is for men who want to find local girls and of course the girls put their details and phone numbers into Punternet. It is the modern version of putting up cards and it provides photos of the girls themselves in lots of detail and not wearing much.

My shop is on a road with plenty of passing cars so its location is good. Also there are shops not too far away so we have pedestrians going past. All this helps. When new faces come in we always ask them where did they see the advertisement. A few give the name of the newsagent or say they saw it on the Internet but a lot say they were just passing. Actually I don't think the answers they give are bound to be true. We always ask if they have been to us before because even if they seem to be new they may have been to the shop before but not on your day.

We have to ask them their names for keeping the books and they are all Dave or John. There are millions of Johns and it has become funny. Some days we would have John, John, John, John in the book throughout a day with maybe just one Dave at the end.

Danger

When you advertise, which of course you must, you are exposing the shop

92

and the girls who work there to an element of danger. There are some weirdoes out there and of course there are the drunks and guys on drugs who are difficult to deal with. Luckily we don't get many of them. We have a security CCTV camera and if they start being awkward I just point to the camera and that usually calms them down. Sometimes I've known men come and push the camera so it's taking in the ceiling and not them. When they come in past the front door there is a reception area where they ring a bell. We have a spy-hole in the second door which is always locked. So the first step is to look at the man on the CCTV and then to check him out again before unlocking the inner door. We feel pretty secure as a result because we could always ring the police if we thought we had a nutter or someone dangerous. Actually the police often pop in to see that everything is OK, not scaring anyone.

I've very seldom experienced real danger in a sauna. Once, though, the place I was working was run by a boss, a very clever woman but she was greedy. I remember five of us girls sitting there. The boss and her son were there too. They had come to collect the money. The door burst open and two guys came in, one white and one black, and I knew straight way that this wasn't right. The white guy came in first and went to the receptionist while the black guy barred the door. He looked like he was high on crack. Then he took out a knife, went to Madam X, the boss, put it to her throat and demanded the money. She was arguing and her son was screaming "give him the bloody money". In the end he got the money off her.

The amazing thing is that I knew that he wasn't going to turn on us. There were five of us girls but he didn't attempt to take our money. It seems like it was a personal thing against Madam X. She was a tough boss and she made a lot of money. You are talking five or six girls to a shift. She had a book full of girls and if you were five minutes late you were told to go home and she called up another one. But she also made very bad enemies and that was her downfall. In the end she got done for a million in tax.

I always said I want to be a nice boss. I would rather have much less than she did and be who I am. I know how the girls used to slag her off behind her back and I wouldn't want that for me although that's human nature.

In terms of being in danger and feeling threatened like the knife attack on Madam X, I've not had that so you could say that a sauna is probably less dangerous to work in than a post office. The risk is there because we deal in cash the whole time and when the sauna business was doing well there was a lot of cash floating around. That's not so these days but it will always be a cash business. I think that the security in my shop is about right.

A different sort of danger I have to deal with is if one of my girls upsets a client, which can happen, and I walk into the situation and have to deal with it. If a girl gets shirty with a client, she doesn't care. It's not her place. I'm the one who gets the threat. They try to scare you by saying people are watching you and you'd better watch yourself. I have had broken windows but I can't be sure whether it was an angry client or kids throwing stones but it makes you aware of your surroundings when you lock up to go home and walk to your car

The police

You'd think the police might be interested in saunas but you don't hear much about raids now. When you do hear of them it is usually somewhere up north, a big operation. In the '70s and '80s we did get raided quite often. They normally leave flats and saunas alone now but I take precautions with my shop. The police used to say that if you were the key holder for the sauna then you were controlling it or managing it. When I leave the shop even now I get the other girls to lock it. If the police were watching the shop they would see different people being "key-holders" so it would be harder to make a case against one person in particular. Some bosses used to make a point of having a cleaner come in first thing and maybe leave last so as to keep themselves in the clear.

Saunas always used to have a receptionist. They would answer the phone and keep punters occupied if all the girls were busy. Sometimes they were ex-working girls and they earned a fixed amount of £50 a shift. That's under £5 an hour. Sometimes the police would say that the receptionist was "controlling" the sauna but that didn't hold up because in reality they were just taking the £10 entrance fee which we always describe as being purely for the massage itself. Anyway, the hard times that saunas are going through mean that most receptionists have gone. We answer the phone calls ourselves and describe ourselves to punters who want to know what we look like. We never say on the phone what we do because if the police were ringing it would give away enough for us to get done. We make a point of not having condoms lying about for the same reason. Girls have locked drawers to keep the condoms or have them in their handbags. If he Bill

94

really went through a sauna they just mustn't find drugs or, of course, foreign girls from East Europe who have been trafficked by pimps and villains.

I've been in a sauna raided by the police just once in all my years and when it happened to me I shat myself. Looking back it was frightening but it was also quite a funny experience. What you've got to remember is when they raid these places they don't want the girls. They want your boss. But obviously you are the bait. They come storming in and take the girls. The punters piss off as best they can and the place gets closed. They take you to the station and a female officer comes in and says: "Look, we know what you do and why you do it. We're not interested in you." And they try to get you to make a statement so that they can get the owner, especially if he's a man, for poncing. Prostitution isn't illegal, but poncing is. So they try to get you to say what you give your boss. You do whatever you like in the room, but the minute you come down and pay your boss, he's poncing.

In my experience the police didn't generally offer to let you off in return for favours but they would waste so much time and money watching the shop. It was not unusual for them to have watched it for about a month or six weeks. Once, we got a tip off from a builder that they were in a flat watching us and he was right. We did get raided.

Sometimes the police liked to do a bit of homework on the girls. They'd try to frighten you. They'd pick up your car registration. They'd find out a little bit about you to scare you and to get you to talk. I wouldn't give a policeman a free service but it's not unusual for them to come in and want it. You think they were just a nice client but when they raid you sometimes you remember them. So the policeman posing as a client would have full sex or whatever he paid for. He wouldn't be able to use that evidence in court, though. The fuckers.

You also got the idiots who came in and showed you their warrant card. They were off-duty policemen so a girl might shit herself and think she had to give him a freebie because he was the Bill. I'd say a lot of girls did that. In my case when I was still new to the game I did one of them once but then I got wise to it and told him, no not you again. I had been told by another policeman who regularly visited the shop that they shouldn't be showing their warrant cards. From then on, when they tried that on me I told them to fuck off because they shouldn't be in there anyway.

95

My own sauna is OK with the police. We've been going for 30 years, we are all mature women, there are no under-age girls and there aren't any complaints. We are absolutely clean on drugs. A couple of years ago we had a plain-clothes copper around to warn us that somewhere else a working girl had been attacked or beaten up and they would warn me. If they were trying to catch some guy or looking for a missing man they might come in and give us a description or a photo-fit to see if we could help. He might have visited the sauna; he might be a loner or a rapist so they ask if we can help. When the police have come to see me it has always been a nice visit up to now. Touch wood, it will always be a nice visit.

If the police were to raid my shop I would tell them truthfully that I am one of the girls who works here, not a madam who comes in and takes money off them. If that happened my nightmare is the consequences. I'm not worried about being locked in a cell but I am frightened of it coming out in the paper. Actually I live a one and a quarter hour drive away so the local paper for the shop isn't sold anywhere near where I live. Most of the girls who work for me also come from quite a way off. I've not been raided in the ten years I've worked in this sauna and it would be sad if it happened. I'm not a big bad madam. I'm just an ordinary working girl trying to make a living. I don't force any of the girls to do what they don't want to do. If they don't want to pay the shift money, they don't have to do the shift because I'll do it myself. Even so, the thought of the repercussions of a raid terrifies the life out of me but it is just something I have to live with.

Chapter 12
WHAT CLIENTS ASK FOR, SOMETIMES GET AND WHAT IT COSTS THEM

Typical clients and why they come

It's not easy to describe a "typical" client if there is such a thing. You could say it is a guy who goes to the room, doesn't ask for any girl in particular or any special service. Maybe he takes a shower and then you take the £10 or £15 massage money off him and go back into the room with him. That's sometimes called the door money. You ask him what he wants and he asks about the prices. Normally you start the tariff with hand relief, full strip hand relief, oral relief which is also known as French, and then sex (meaning fucking) which is sometimes combined with French. Those are the basic services that a girl reels off. The normal client will pick one of those services.

Massage with hand relief is £40 and then it goes up in tens. Your topless or full strip is £50, sex is £60 or £70 and you may throw a little bit of French in with it. French and sex in my sauna are always done with a condom so far as I'm concerned. But if a guy offers the girl another £30 or so she may give him a bit of French without a condom so he is looking at £100.

In my sauna a client pays £15 for the massage and £15 for the sauna. If he doesn't want anything else he would get five minutes on his back and five on his front. Not much more. Very few clients bother with the sauna but just a few do. In the cold weather some like it. The £15 is not an entrance fee though some places call it that. In reality it is a massage to get him excited so that he wants to get on with the French and sex. The sooner you can get him to come, the better. When he has come, we wipe him up with tissues and normally he gets dressed and goes. Sometimes he takes a shower to make sure there is no smell of massage oil or powder on him. Of course we never wear perfume for the obvious reason that he may be on his way home.

Half an hour or a bit less from first to last is normally right for your typical client. That includes undressing and dressing. You tell him that if he wants more time, say an hour, then you double the price but with the second half-hour cheaper. Not many clients want a full hour. If you do your job well you make them happy in half an hour. Actually, the ones who say they just want a massage and hand-relief are more tricky to handle than the ones who just want sex. The guy has paid the minimum price but while you stand there wanking him off his hand is up your skirt, he's trying to get into your fanny, he's over your tits and can he do this, can he do that? And you say, yes just a little bit and you are thinking if I let him do that he might come quicker. But you realise that this service is going into another service level.

If the client just wants straight-forward sex you know what you are doing. You give him French and then he has sex. Six out of ten of the ones who say they just want hand relief will try to take liberties. About half of clients are happy to come with just hand relief or oral. The others want a bit of all three finishing with sex.

The ones who want sex mainly go for missionary or doggie style, but some of them want all sorts of positions, on and off the table. We often call them Heinz 57 Varieties! Actually a massage table is not that big and that's a difference from flats where girls have ordinary beds. The position that is hardest work is when the client is on his back and the girl rides on top of him facing either way. It starts getting on your nerves. You think, I've gone this way and that way and now he wants me on top. This means you have to do the hard work and he just lies there while you sweat away and he's staring at you. I find that very personal and I get off straight away and change the mood.

The perfect client is the one who comes in, gets missionary position, goes boom-boom-boom and he's gone. That can take as little as two minutes from the time his cock gets into you to the time he's come. Of course plenty of men have erections that last much longer and some can hold their orgasm back to keep it all going. Some will tell you he's just had a wank or had a Viagra. Or if he's just had a drink that may slow him down. Others do poppers to keep it going a little longer. We don't have poppers in the shop but I can't stop what they have in their pockets, so if they want to go into the toilet and do a popper that's up to them. It may be great for the man to have another ten minutes while he's being wanked but it's no good for the girl when she's standing there sweating and she's only going to get £40

98

at the end of it.

Clients come in all ages from about 30 to 70 or even more. It's rare to get clients in their 20s but when it happens I think it may just be out of curiosity or they are highly sexed. Sometimes the ones in their 20s are young Asian guys. Clients have all sorts of educational backgrounds. A lot say they are builders or salesmen.

When a man goes out of the door and says he is going to work you never know where he is going and he may be coming in to see us. Lunch-breaks, tea-breaks or travelling after meetings, some of our clients don't have much time. It leaves the niggling feeling that my man could be doing that as well. That's the difficulty. If they didn't want to come and see us, we'd have no business, so they have to lie. There aren't many men who will go round saying that they spent the afternoon with a working girl.

A few clients in my shop — less than a handful — are disabled. We have a guy in a wheel chair and a guy on a zimmer who had a stroke. And there's a guy who comes in who is deaf. Some of them are awful. One is incontinent and he's moody too but he's a likeable dirty old man. He's getting on and could be near eighty. He wants hand relief. He thinks he has come and he hasn't. We used to be in the room with him for an hour sweating but now after a certain amount of time we say "Jim, you've really come" and he thinks he has. He pays well but we have to work for it. He smells awful. We have to undress him, we have to shower him, we have to watch he doesn't fall and it's a half-hour process before you get him in the room. Then you have to get him dressed and call him a taxi. When he's gone the place smells of piss. All the girls in my place know him and when he rings up they all say "Oh no, not Jim". I do find that people with disabilities are very, very difficult. And they don't pay more. It's a kind of social service that we provide for them.

In the room all clients like to chat and we chat them up to make them feel relaxed, particularly if they are new to the place. You go into the room and say, "Hello, what's your name?" More often than not it's John or Dave. Let's call him John. John opens up the conversation with "How long have you been doing this? or "What made you get into this?" That's a question they find interesting. I think "Here we go". Sometimes I have a sarcastic reply on the tip of my tongue but I can't use it because you are always wanting to get money out of this guy. There is one reason and one reason only why we are in the business. Money.

Still the answer I give and I think most girls do is to say "It was a friend who told me about it, or it was a friend who was working as a receptionist who suggested I should do it." None of us will go any deeper by saying: "Well, as a matter of fact I was abused as a child or I really enjoy having sex" After that they fire random questions at you. "Where do you live...are you married...have you got any kids?" Sometimes this starts getting our backs up and I think "fuck me, you come in here for a massage and you start trying to get the story of my life." Really I think many of them are just nervous, the first-timers, that is.

I now have a knack of turning that round and I say to them "So why do you come in here then?" Mostly they don't answer that question. Or if they do, they are still having to cope with the initial shock that I have thrown the question back at them. Then you get all sorts of stories. A typical one is "I'm not from round here. I'm just working up here for a couple of weeks". The other standard one is "I don't sleep with my wife". Others in the same group are "I don't get on with my wife or I've just got divorced". I've even had some outrageous ones like his missus was giving birth so that's why he has come in. I've even had clients come in from a funeral!

Some clients are probably telling the truth when they say their wives or partners won't do particular things they want. It's sexual frustration. The partner won't give them oral or let them give oral or give and receive oral at once, which is known as Sixty-Nine. I think that there are a lot of women out there who won't. They've been married 20 years and never given their husbands a blow-job. Men love receiving oral and a lot come in just for that. I think that was definitely the case a few generations ago and it is still true now. I've been told that the reason that women started wearing lipstick in Roman times was to show that they were working girls who were willing to do oral.

In a sauna the girls lie to the clients and the clients lie to the girls. It's obvious when you think about it. When a girl leaves the shop she will be wearing jeans and a loose sweater. Her hair will be pulled back and she won't be looking anything glamorous or out of the ordinary. She has two compartmentalised lives and she keeps them completely separate. She has a working name in the sauna and a real name in the outside world. She'll mainly call the other girls by their working names. Clients often ask the girl

100

what her real name is and mentally she'll tell him to fuck off. She doesn't ask him if John or Dave is his real name, does she!

To be a working girl is thought of as shameful in the outside world. Inside the sauna where every girl is a working girl you are at ease. You make friendships with other working girls, a few of which can last a long time. You almost never make any sort of friendship with clients, even with regulars who may come and see you every month or even every week for years. I've only known a tiny number of cases when a girl liked a client enough to let him take her on holiday, all expenses paid of course, and she could join up with his other friends without giving anything away. But that's the exception.

Working girls may sometimes take holidays together and go to sunny places abroad. This was common when the sauna business was good but isn't happening much now. The golden rule is you don't mix your two lives and you are really discreet about the clients who come and what you do for them. In the back of their minds must be the worry of them being found out or shopped to their wives.

The world of working girls, bosses and pimps is always on the edge of the law and this means that a working girl trusts nobody. Certainly not the clients however generous and kind. As for trusting other girls, that takes time. It's sad to have to go through life trusting almost nobody but it comes with the job. If you choose the job you put up with the consequences.

Being a working girl makes it difficult, almost impossible, to trust a man. If I had had a different life, met my Mr Right, had had 2.3 children and my house and my little car in the drive I would never have known if my husband was a little shit, that he visited saunas or anything about them. Maybe that's the world I should be in.

I've had women ringing me in the shop who have found out something about the shop and that their husbands have been going there. I try and lie to them but normally that doesn't get you anywhere. I remember one time a woman rang my shop and spoke to one of the girls. There was a big panic because she mentioned one of my girls by name. I don't know how she had found out about her husband but she wanted to speak to the boss. So I took the phone. I was on the defensive but I felt terribly sorry for her. To begin with she was very angry and she was desperate. But she wasn't shouting at me, she wasn't horrible. She was well spoken and intelligent and she knew that at first I was lying and covering up until I just felt I couldn't do this.

She wanted to know what the girl looked like and what things we did. I could hear that she was begging, dying to know that her husband wasn't having an affair or going to leave her. She was relieved to know that the girl in question wasn't a young dollybird but was probably older than her. That's why I invited her to the place. It was a long conversation at the end of which she calmed down and became very nice. I kept saying to her, "It's not what you think. Your husband isn't having an affair and we are basically just here for the money." I said she could come round and see us if she wanted. She didn't come but she let me know she was grateful to me for talking with her and making her understand there was no affair going on because all we want is the money. At the end of the conversation she was very calm and she thanked me. I guess her man had some explaining to do.

I expect that at least half the clients I see are cheating on someone. There must be thousands, millions of men out there who don't come to see working girls. They get their sex for free and the lucky ones have partners who give them everything they want so they don't need to cheat. Sometimes I think that even when a man has a woman who does everything we can do and it doesn't cost him he may still cheat just for the sake of novelty. There are plenty of swingers clubs where men can swap partners and the women like it too. The difference in the service that working girls provide is that both sides know what they want. The man gets his buzz, the girl gets her money and both sides are happy. It doesn't take long and it doesn't entail emotion and tears. It may not be a perfect solution to solving men's sexual needs, but it's a good one.

Personally, I have always been completely faithful to my partners. It sounds odd when you think that I am being fucked three or four times a day for money but it's true. It happens quickly and it gives me no physical pleasure though I have to pretend it does. My partner and I still have a good time in bed together. My partner has to be accepting of what I am from the word go. It's my chosen profession; it pays the rent and for bringing up my kids. I've never been dependent on others except when I was ill, and my partners have lived off me much more than I have lived off them. I've never been a supported or a kept woman.

Being a working girl means that the trust that is a big part of traditional relationships has to be sacrificed. Rule one in the business is never get involved with clients and never trust them. Sadly that spills over to never trusting anyone, not even partners. How can I be sure that my partner isn't some other girl's punter?

In my 20 years as a working girl there has only been one client who first became a regular and little by little became a friend who I could trust. Just one.

Regulars and passing trade

A sauna is a business like lots of other small businesses. We like to have as many regular clients as possible but passing trade is vital too. This is why saunas like to be on a street or road with passing cars, pedestrians and maybe close to some conventional retail shops. Men in cars need to be able to see our sign which says "Sauna and massage". They need to be able to park somewhere inconspicuous nearby such as in a residential road and they need to be able walk into the sauna quickly. My sauna has the standard layout of a front door which is always unlocked when the sauna is open, a waiting room or foyer with a locked inner door and a bell. The client can see if the foyer is vacant the moment he pushes the front door open. If he sees a client waiting there he is likely to turn away quickly because men don't like to sit in what is like a doctor's waiting room eyeing each other. This means that the moment we hear the inner doorbell ring one of the girls goes to answer it. She will check the internal CCTV monitor and look through the spy-hole. Then she will open the door quickly.

A small sauna like mine will have two or three massage rooms so the girl wants to get the client into one of them as quickly as possible. With a known regular, that is easy. We just make the client feel welcome by telling him how nice it is to see him again and we make a point of remembering his name if we can.

To anyone who we think is new we always begin with "Have you been here before?" We sometimes get evasive answers such as "Quite a long time ago". If the client has been before he will know what to expect and may remember the girl's name. If he says it's his first time we say: "That's nice. How did you hear about us?" From this we try to work out whether our advertising is working. A few clients will say "From the newsagent" or "I saw you on the Internet". Commonly they say I was walking or driving past, which comes back to the importance of the sauna's location.

With girls who work from their own flats the position is quite different. Most actually live in their flats though some are rented purely as working premises. Since the flats are always in residential areas they have to be more discreet than saunas. Saunas can show their face to the public and the public can make its own guesses about what goes on inside. In a residential block of flats neighbours will notice if there is a steady flow of men ringing the bell of a particular flat. Also, from the girl's point of view, if she lives in the flat the more clients she has the greater the risk that they will come along drunk and ring her bell when she doesn't want to be working anyway.

When the doorbell rings and we have had a quick look to see who has rung it, one of the girls goes to open it at once. In our place we take it in turns to open for clients. The CCTV camera is above the door and looking downwards so we sometimes cannot recognize regulars. The spy-hole in the door is better for that, so the camera and the video it makes and stores for 24 hours is more to protect ourselves in emergencies. It has the other use of enabling the boss to check how many clients have come in a shift and to see that the girls aren't "knocking the shop" by not recording them and pocketing the shift money.

Once the client has come through the inner door and we have asked the standard questions, we take him to an available room and ask him what he wants. At this point he will ask what we do and what it costs. That takes just a minute or two. If the service has been agreed we take the £15 off him at once or, if we have doubts about the man, we will ask for full payment for what has been agreed. Then we offer him a cup of tea or coffee and ask if he wants to take a shower. We give him five minutes to get undressed and another five minutes or so if he is taking a shower too. Then we bring him the cup of tea and the service begins.

If the guy is a regular he will say the name of the girl he wants. If she is in and free, he will get her. If she is busy with another client we put him in an empty room and we tap on the door of the girl he wants to inform her that she has a client waiting.

If two girls go to the door at the same time the client gets a choice. He eyes them up and down and the girls wear black underwear beneath their white overalls so the client gets a good sight of their bras, panties, hold-ups and

104

legs. We have to dress to please and we get used to being eyed by clients. It's not too bad and comes with the job. If you don't like it you shouldn't be in the game.

When the place is quiet this introduction routine is straightforward but as so often happen you wait for ages and then two or three clients call in within a half hour. We don't want them to meet up in the showers or the loo because they would be embarrassed, so sometimes we have to juggle things a bit, letting one into the shower or the loo and then getting another client out of the massage room and out of the front door. At times like these we may have two clients in adjacent massage rooms being done at the same time. We have a stereo radio playing outside the rooms to cover up conversations and other noises in the rooms.

Sometimes organising two clients being worked on in different rooms at the same time requires some skill. If both girls are working and the doorbell goes one of us has to slip a white coat over whatever we have on at the time, which may be nothing at all, go to the inner door and put our heads round. In these circumstances we have to say that both girls are working and can he come back in 30 minutes. We hate to lose clients this way but equally we have to make the clients in the massage rooms feel that they are getting their money's worth and are not being rushed. Hence, the key is to make the client come as quickly as possible without making him feel rushed.

The reason that regular clients are such a blessing is because we remember what they like. For example they may like us to talk dirty while we wank them off or they fuck us and of course we have to pretend we enjoy being fucked. Hence smiles, jokes and laughter are part of our stock in trade whatever we really are feeling like at the time. Girls who just lie back on the massage table without responding and acting a bit will never convert new clients into regulars.

Long term clients

Remembering clients' faces and names is a big plus in any job and we are no exception. Of course the name is probably not the real one but that doesn't matter. Clients need to feel welcome and these days they bloody well are. I'm pretty good at names and faces and I am very good at being bubbly and fun. It's been part of my real nature since a kid and now it comes naturally to me when I am in my working girl persona. I can be a different woman at home with the usual ups and downs of family life.

Though I may not remember much about a particular client when he's at the door, when I go into the room quite often something clicks back from my subconscious memory. Things they do in the room, things they say, certain mannerisms can remind me of what they wanted last time.

Another way is for me to give them nicknames. If the client comes regularly to the place and will go with any of the girls we share these nicknames. When we say the nickname of a client who has just come in, the other girls know plenty about him, good and bad. We gossip a lot about what clients like and the ones who are difficult. We like it and we have so much time in our parlour between clients that gossip is fun. With some clients who always want me, I just use the nickname in my own memory. Also I may not say anything about what his particular buzz is, for example if he likes to wear stockings or be caned. After all, if he is my regular why should I make it easy for other girls to give him the fun that I do?

In a small shop like ours the girls are generally good at not poaching other girls' regulars, but if the regular's favourite girl isn't working that day it is much better that another girl does him and gets the money. These days we can't afford to send any client away if we can avoid it. A regular is like gold-dust these days. I have had regulars come to me over ten years in my sauna and there are other girls who have had a few regulars for fifteen or even 20 years. A regular is a potential stream of cash in the pocket.

Regulars don't always stay anything like that long. Some of my regulars disappear for a bit. I'm sure they are going off to see other girls and trying out different things. Or they start going to a flat and getting it cheaper. Then they may come back and think they can get the same service in the sauna. You always know when they have been travelling around because they come with different ideas.

The term regular goes back many years to when saunas were really busy and regulars would come every week. Things aren't that way anymore but if a client comes once every three months you still class him as a regular to the place. As for weekly regulars they are far fewer now.

Since regulars are right down now, new men ringing the doorbell are even more important. I learn to size them up pretty quickly. I don't turn many

106

away but as it's all about money I find that a lot of Asians get turned away because they want it for next to nothing. All girls may have to bargain a bit with a new client and will only drop their prices if they are having a bad day. Some clients you ask to leave because they are just too difficult and piss you off. Some ask for things you aren't prepared to do like sex or oral without a condom and you just tell them to go. If there is something about them you don't like or you feel uncomfortable with them, you just don't do them.

About seven out of 10 of my clients are regulars and the others are passing clients and I'd say that applies to the shop as a whole. My shop has always been heavily dependent on regular clients. A few of my long-term clients go back as far as 15 years and have come with me when I have changed sauna. A few of them, about five, have my mobile number as well as that of the shop. I've given it them so that they can ring me to make sure I am going to be in the shop when they want to come. It's a risk that they may abuse things by ringing me at bad times or sending dirty text messages, but again in my present financial position I have to take some chances to keep really good long-term clients.

Even long-term clients of 10 years or more know virtually nothing about me and I know little about them. I don't really enjoy chat in the massage room. For me it is a business. I don't go there to look for a man. I don't go there to look for a partner. I don't go there to look for sex. I go there for money. That applies to all the girls.

Sometimes we talk about star signs and the dates of birthdays may come up. I don't let on about my birthday even if I thought they might give me a present or extra money. I find that too personal. A birthday is a special day and I don't want to share it with a client.

Working girls all want to keep their two lives completely apart. Some of us use two mobiles, one for our work and the other for the rest of our life. It's a good system if you use pay-as-you-go.

Chapter 13
SERVICES THAT SAUNA GIRLS MAY OFFER

Basics: hand relief, oral and fucking

The basics that we offer are hand relief, oral and fucking. It may seem surprising but hand relief can be hard work and I think that most girls would prefer to put the condom on and to suck and fuck. It's not always the case but sometimes the clients who take the longest are the ones wanting hand relief. Some of them are older but I think other ones know that it takes longer with hand relief than with fucking and they like that. Some say, "I only want hand relief and I'll give you £40 because I know I'm going to come quick". If it works out like that, it's OK because why should they pay you £80 for something that is over in a few seconds. A client who fucks me comes in less than five minutes hopefully.

With oral you have to know what you are doing because you are doing the work and the client is just lying there. You get to learn how to bring him off. If it isn't happening you have to step it up the pace until you know he has come. I look at it like this. If I am in the room for more than 20 minutes I am doing something wrong. You have to give the client the feeling that you are not rushing him even though you are. There are all sorts of different ways you can do that and the longer you work the more you get it down to a fine art. You come out and you look at the clock. You've only been fifteen minutes but the client doesn't realise he's only been fifteen minutes. You learn how to rush it but to slow it down in a funny sort of way.

When the girl does oral for the man, that is what we call French. When the guy comes that way we call it a blowjob or BJ for short. It's something that most men love and they ask for it because they can't get their partners at home to do it for them. A joke we have when we hear a police car siren outside is to say "He's on a promise" meaning that he wants to get home fast because his partner has promised him a blowjob!

Reverse oral or 69 is absolutely standard now. Some years ago you would say to the client that straight sex was £50. He'd say, "can I go down on you?" and you'd say "OK but that's an extra tenner or twenty". Now that times are hard you let them do that as part of the package that you agree for the fee. I'd say that five clients out of ten want to go down on me. As for me, I don't get anything from it. It's my job. It's part and parcel of my service.

69 is when the client is on his back on the table. I get up there facing the other way with my pussy on his mouth. If he's got a condom on I'll oral him while he's sucking me. Otherwise he gets hand relief. I charge extra for 69 — a tenner or twenty if I can. It takes more effort from me and I definitely look on it as an extra service.

Kissing

'French', which means sucking a man's cock, mustn't be confused with French kissing which means putting your tongue into the client's mouth and him doing the same to you. On Punternet, when girls list the services they offer, French kissing may not be one of them. Some may have worries about catching Herpes or Aids but for many of us kissing is what we reserve for our boyfriends and partners. We feel it to be much more intimate than being fucked, which may seem funny but really is the case. We feel as if our faces are out of bounds. Some of my clients kiss me lightly on the lips and that's OK though I don't encourage it. One of my special clients, Inspector Gadget, kisses my lips and face a lot and I let him do it because he really cares for me but he's an exception.

For me, my face is a no-go area to ordinary clients. Some of them ask if they can wank themselves off and shoot all over my face. I just say no. I know some girls let them do it but for me it would be degrading so it doesn't happen.

Breast relief

Breast relief is something that comes up quite a bit. Some girls call it body to body. I don't mind doing it but it's not one of my favourites. I'm not particularly busty anyway so I'm not known for my boobs. They are not an asset of mine and I haven't made my money with boobs. You'll find that girls who are busty cater for that service a lot better and get asked for that more. My way of doing it is for me to lie down and push my tits together while he is on top. So he puts his cock between them and comes like that. I don't offer it when I am asked what I do but I will do it if he asks. Sometimes if I am doing hand relief with a full strip I might incorporate it at the end but this can be with the client on his back. Then I stroke his cock with my tits and can cup them together round his cock for a bit. I'll consider anything that makes him come quicker and gives him an extra thrill so that he will come back again. If I start wanking him off and he starts talking about tits, you know he's got a thing about them so you use them round his cock. If he starts playing with mine you know he's a tits man.

When I was pregnant and still working my tits got large and I had some clients who loved tit relief. I did it OK because I knew I was going to need the money. After the baby came and when I went back to work one client in particular loved to see me squirt milk from my tits.

Everything about the job is about sending the client off with a smile on his face in the least possible time. You want him back soon and regularly so finding out how to please each client is the secret of being a successful working girl. Once he's come he's happy. There are a few who say to you they want to come twice. When they do I just say the price is double because I know that the second time is going to be twice as hard. Normally they find they can't do it but if they've paid me double money that's OK.

Anal

Anal is something that quite a lot of men ask about and we get them asking about it on the phone. Some girls offer it as a service. As a boss I always say that they have to discuss it privately with the girl. I've done it plenty of times but I would never OK it over the phone. I would have to see them and obviously I would have to see how big they were. There are a couple of guys who come to the shop regularly and want anal. They get it and yes I'm willing to do it – with a condom of course. They pay really well.

Water sports

Water sports are when the client wants you to pee on him or he wants to pee on you. I've peed on clients. That's OK. I have let a client pee on me but I don't like it. For me it is degradation and now I draw the line there and I don't do it. In a sauna you have a shower room so peeing on a client is easy enough.

111

There was a client who I used to visit. He was an old guy, a war veteran who lived in Chelmsford. I used to visit him every two weeks like clockwork. In some ways he was a bit gone as a result of being in the war and he was very old. When he saw my car pulling round the corner he always used to shout out "Thar she blows" He is the only guy I know who drank literally every drop of my piss. Before I left I had to piss in a jug and leave it for him to drink. I think that during the war he drank piss. He was about 90 years old. That's all I had to do for him.

In the shop it's OK in the shower room because the floor can be mopped and disinfected.

Spanking and caning

Spanking and caning are something that quite a lot of men enjoy. I don't mind doing it but I won't have it on me. I don't want to be whipped or caned. I just don't like pain. I'll inflict it though. Quite a few clients want it. It's not something I get asked for every day. Some clients want spanking just with the hand. Others want the cane or the slipper. I have a guy who pays me £30 to give him twelve strokes and then runs out of the door. Twelve strokes with the cane. He pulls his pants up, throws me £30 and runs out. I do it hard and it leaves marks. I find it is mainly the old boys who like this. It's a certain generation, perhaps in their 50s or maybe older. In the shop we keep a cane, a slipper and a paddle. Sometimes the client wants dressing up to so we have glamour wear, small girl wear and vibrators. The dressing up wear can be used by us or the clients.

The spanking or caning sessions are specialised as far as we are concerned. They generally finish up with hand relief or they wank themselves. Some want to end up with a fuck but for most of them fucking's not their buzz.

BDSM and role play

BDSM is becoming more mainstream these days. When you go into Ann Summers you see all sorts of equipment including kits for beginners, and the people who are looking at them are quite often couples in their twenties or thirties. In the past I used to be asked to wear BDSM gear at the light end of the scene such as shiny black costumes and bras with holes for the nipples. I've had some funky clients who have brought stuff into saunas for me to wear. I don't do that now. I find it a bit too dark for me. I don't mind dressing up as a school girl providing it doesn't go over a certain level. I've got kids so I don't like it if they start talking about their daughters. It may be them fantasising but I just don't like it. I can pretend I am fourteen but there's a limit I can go to before I shut that off.

I've known girls who have gone much further and worked in dungeons. It fucks them up. A lot of sniffing poppers goes on in that scene and you find the mistresses in the dungeons are into it, not just the clients. I knew a girl who used to get tied up for hours and sometimes it went on all night. She earned good money but she was always popping and pilling and at the end of it she was shattered. It fucked her up.

It doesn't happen in my place. I can't control it if clients bring in poppers in their pockets. They leave a smell but in half an hour it has gone.

Two girls at once

Some guys ask for a two-girl massage and then the big question is what do I get? The answer is you get what you pay for. For example, if you want to fuck both of us, it is £60 each. If you see them humming and hawing you say, well I won't quite hold you to the £60 each. So you go for the £50 each or even £40 each if it's a bad day. Two-girl massages work brilliantly if you are working with the right girl because you can wrap it up fast. If you both know the client you know how to make him come quick.

Two or more men at once

In the past I have had two men at once but not in the sauna. It was more likely to be at a party that was arranged, an orgy. Girls like us would be invited. There would be a bit of coke. We would get paid a fixed amount to attend and to do anyone who came. So there were times that I would end up in a room doing two guys at the same time, one in the mouth and one in the pussy. I have had double penetration (DP) — one in the pussy and one in the bum at the same time — but not often. I did it professionally a few times and got paid very well for it but I didn't like it so I stopped and haven't done it again.

Two men at once doesn't really happen in my shop. I don't say it couldn't or mustn't but basically the guys who come in want to do their own thing. The massage rooms aren't designed for two guys. They just have a massage table and not a lot of room otherwise. You wouldn't find it easy to have two men fucking the girl at once. I think they would be better to go to specialised parties for that sort of thing. They are advertised in Punternet. I wouldn't want to get involved.

Orgies and bukake

I've known about orgies and swinging parties for ages of course. There are plenty around and a lot are commercially organised. You find them on Punternet and there are plenty of private clubs to cater for swingers. Some of them specialise in BDSM but I have never been.

Many people think that if you are a working girl anything goes. I am a faithful woman and I can't really have sex with someone, apart from professionally and for money, unless I am in love with him. Swinging parties and orgies don't appeal to me. I am a one-to-one person. What I do for a job is one thing. My life outside that job is completely different.

Bukake is a Japanese invention. One girl services a group of men by sucking them in turn. She may get two cocks in her mouth at once and certainly she will use both hands to wank two other guys at the same time. They don't use condoms. This is a big attraction for the men and the girl must have made up her mind that the risk is OK. The men are allowed to come in her mouth or over her face. To me all that is dangerous and degrading and I wouldn't do it whatever the money. I suppose that just as lots of men love sucking pussy or "muff-diving" there must be some girls who actually get a buzz from doing oral and bukake. If not they could just choose to do the usual things in a sauna or a flat.

There can be a lot more money in a short time from bukake. If the girl does 10 men at the same time in an hour for £50 each she gets £500 less the cost of the hotel room which might be £100. £400 for one hour's work sounds great but she really has to work hard for it. I wonder her neck doesn't get stiff with all that sucking. I still think that the risks she takes of catching Herpes or whatever are crazy. It's known as "oral without" or OWO for short. A lot of girls won't do oral without a condom ever. I'm really quite an old-fashioned working girl and I think that the younger ones who do these things are storing up a lot of trouble for themselves.

114

Celebrity clients

During my 20 years as a working girl I have done a good number of celebrities. It is obvious that I cannot name them because they would sue the publishers of this book. Also if working girls started spilling the beans about their clients, even ordinary clients would feel threatened and this would damage the business. We need to protect them. Clients want to be anonymous. In the shop we have a CCTV camera above the door and it is not quite out of reach. Sometime we find that clients have reached up to push it out of the way so that it doesn't film them. That's how they feel. Maybe they think they'll get blackmailed.

What I can say is that quite a number of my clients have been prominent household names. There was a comedian, various footballers, a concert violinist, a Labour peer who was regularly in the news during Tony Blair's time as prime minister, actors and top judges. You would have thought that such people would be terrified of putting their reputations on the line for the tabloid papers to put through the wringer. In fact I think that mainly these people will use escorts from agencies working out of posh hotels. Escorts are much more expensive, starting on £150 to £300 for an hour but when you are a footballer on £50 grand a week, that money is peanuts.

With footballers you just think, they've got so much cash and nobody thinks much of them as people off the pitch anyway. With top judges, musicians, actors and the like I find I do laugh to myself to think of what the public would say if they knew the truth. One of the things is that some of these people who are top earners by any standards are mean when it comes to paying for sex. One well known comedian would come to see me regularly. One day he left his watch in the room so I put it safely in a drawer for the next time he came. It wasn't anything special and had just a quartz movement. Not a Rolex or anything. But he made such a big fuss about this watch that might have been worth £30. OK, perhaps it had sentimental value but to me it seemed all part of his cheapness and it amused me to see this successful comedian on the box who was a cheap-skate client cribbing about a £30 watch.

Footballers are a group who I find cocky. They have so much money it makes them blasé. There have been cases in the papers where football clubs have organised Christmas parties in hotels for their players and have invited working girls. For us that's OK if the money is right but it also means that

115

the players think that the public doesn't mind if they come along to use our services. Wayne Rooney was in the papers some time ago before he got married for visiting a sauna and sitting there chatting with other clients. He was laying himself open for trouble. Most clients don't want to be seen by other guys even though they all know what they are there for.

Politicians are a different bunch. I always find them a bit creepy. They are the ones who are more likely to wear frilly underwear, stockings and do posing in mirrors. They are eye-openers. I look on them as quite dark and they have things up their sleeves. Compare them with what I might call a normal client. He comes in off the building site or from the office. He goes for a pee. "Seventy quid, love". Boom, boom. You know where you are. Washes his hands. "See you later, darling". That's what I call a normal client, an ideal client.

But politicians and judges are a bit funky, a bit far out, weird. I have written things on judges chests in break time and they have gone back to sentence someone with obscenities written all over their chest. And these were top judges in the Old Bailey sending people down for whatever but they are sitting in court and underneath their cloaks I know what is written because I wrote it with a marker pen.

One judge had a particular thing. He was old and pushing seventy or eighty. I don't know if he had come out of retirement. I was working in London at the time. His shoes were heavy. My job was to take his shoe off, tie it to his balls and kick it. I used to keep kicking it for half an hour. He never came. He would have two of us and would pay top money. We just had to stand there in high heels. We would take it in turns to kick the shoe, then we would write all over him in marker pen and then he would go back to court.

With your normal client you are just using your fanny. After that it isn't the same because you are using your head and you have to work that little bit harder. You have to use your mental agility as well as your physical side. Sometimes you've just done a client and the next one comes in with his carrier bag. He has all sorts of gadgets in it and he wants you to use this, use that, do this, do that. Then he wants to wear your knickers, put your stockings on. It's not straight forward and you always find it's those clients that don't want to pay much. Every girl has clients like that. Every place has clients like that. The others always pay what we ask as our proper rate.

116

The man next door, the builder, the plumber will pay. They are the ones we like. They are what the job is all about. They are easy money.

When you have to use your mental agility it drains you. He wants to dress up. He wants you to dress up. Then he wants to watch you wee or to watch him pee or he wants to come in the shower with you. That's hard work.

She-male sauna "girls"

These days trans-gender people are more common that they used to be. There are transvestites who get their buzz from dressing up like girls but they don't go further than that and in their normal life are seen to be men. Then there are the men who've been through the long and painful change with surgery, hormone treatment and the rest of it. I'm talking about a much smaller group sometimes called she-males. You can see photos of them on the internet. Basically they look like lovely women with feminine faces, nice boobs, slim wrists, no Adam's apple and they still have a cock. In my working life I have come across just two of them who were working "girls".

I also came across a transvestite guy who was an electrician. I rang a boss I was working for and asked him if he knew an electrician. He said he did and he'd send me one. The guy came to the door with his box of tools and in woman's clothes but I could see it was a man. He turned out to be a blindingly good electrician but it was funny watching him go up ladders in stockings, miniskirts and high heels. Obviously if he got called out to ordinary people he couldn't do that, but if he got called out to the sauna that is what he liked to do. Then when he'd fixed whatever it was he would hang around in the sauna wanting to be with the girls because he felt like a girl and he could be what he wanted to be. When he went up a ladder he'd like people to see him up there. Men looking up his skirt were a buzz for him for him and the clients probably enjoyed it even though they could see he was a transvestite.

Carolina, the she-male

Carolina was very very beautiful. Long curly black hair, very tall, very glamorous. She worked with us at Madam X's place. We were on alternating shifts so you were never on a shift with the same girls and there was a different rota every week. When it came to my week working with

117

her, I had heard through the receptionist what the girls had started saying: she was a man and when I asked her she admitted it. She was a man, with a willy. She had beautiful boobs and if she hadn't told you she was a man you wouldn't have known. The voice wasn't that of a man. There was nothing to detect a man whatever.

I don't know if she was going through treatment. Gender change people have all sorts of treatment before the operation. I don't think she was and as far as working was concerned she knew she could get away with it despite the cock because she looked so good, better than anyone. I think she had a way of tucking her cock back between her legs. To this day I do not know how she did it. All I know is that she did men, she made money and she was popular. She lived in North London and used to advertise for herself working from her flat and she was rolling in money. How she did sex I don't know. I wonder if the clients did anal or went in there thinking it was pussy. All I know is she got away with it. When the other girls in the sauna found out they didn't feel threatened; they just thought it was hilarious. We found her fascinating because she was busier than anyone else in there. Actually she moved on very soon so I didn't have the chance to swap life histories.

There was another working girl, slim blonde and very pretty who was also a man. I met her in another sauna and then she branched out on her own. She was very well known and I think that she was known to have a willy. Maybe that was a special thing that clients wanted to see and try out. In the sauna s/he worked as a working girl. Privately in her own flat she worked as a she-male.

Of the hundreds of working girls I have known in my career, only two had willies.

Chapter 14
CLIENTS WITH SPECIAL REQUIREMENTS

The great majority of clients want ordinary sex in some form, whether fucking, oral or hand relief. I look on them as being straight-forward clients. Others want some extras that are easy to do and give them pleasure as well as enabling me to charge a higher fee. Some like me to dress up for them. My standard uniform is the white coat that I wear when they first arrive at the sauna. This helps us to preserve the fiction that the sauna is a place to get a therapeutic massage like being done by a physio or an osteopath. It heightens the game for the client if he gets a glimpse of black underwear and black hold-ups when he arrives, particularly for the first time.

Some like me to dress like a schoolgirl: white blouse and short navy skirt. I sometimes wonder about this. I like to think that they can work their fantasy out with me and that doing so will keep them away from school kids. I think any form of actual paedophilia is offensive and vile. After all, I was abused myself as a kid by Uncle Nick.

A few want to be caned, generally not very hard, and the shop has one on hand when needed. Others like to me to push my finger up their bum. I do this wearing a condom on one hand and wanking the client off with the other. It clearly heightens their pleasure. They may also like me to use toys such as vibrators on them. The Rampant Rabbit is a best seller at Ann Summers's shops. Some men bring their own including the massage cream they particularly like. To me these are all enhancements — the sort of thing that many couples of all ages will do together anyway. The reason that many men come to saunas is because working girls will do the things that their partners won't do.

Anal sex is a kind of dividing line. Some girls will do it. Some including me normally won't unless the guy is quite small and the money is right: at least £100. I am a bit tight there and it can painful even with plenty of KY jelly. Again, I have nothing against it and I have always done it a bit in the past if the money was right.

119

But there is a range of "special requests" that I'd say aren't natural and which only crop up now and then. If I can satisfy the client I do them and the stranger they are the more money he has to pay. Anyway, here goes.

Noel, the transvestite

Noel was a regular which in those days meant once a week. I had met him in Madam X's sauna. He was local to the sauna and we were within 20 minutes of each other. I had done visiting before and for me it was a bonus on my days off from the sauna. Madam X didn't know, so the £80 were all mine as opposed to paying out £30 to Madam X.

Noel worked in a department store and he got discounts there. He was always buying me presents, mainly perfumes: Cartier, Chanel. I would go to his place and he always paid me £80. He wanted a special service and I've never come across one like him. He never wanted sex. He lived alone. He always had his curtains drawn even during the day. You might say he was bordering on weird. I didn't find him weird because I got to know him. He was troubled, I think, but he was a nice guy.

Noel was a guy who had to plan and prepare. He would never ring me out of the blue and say can you come tonight? He would prepare for a few days. He was a transvestite and he was into it big time. He had a wardrobe full of clothes and shoes. You've never seen so many shoes in your life. High-heel patent black, red, yellow. Beautiful shoes everywhere.

He also used to smother every single wall in his bedroom with filthy photos. The walls were covered from corner to corner with girls from the girlie mags. This takes days to prepare and that is what he used to do. When I had gone he would take them all down.

On the bed there would be one sheet laid out. Perfectly ironed, immaculate, one crisp clean white sheet. It was a ritual. I knew what I had to do when I went in. He would always open the door to me in high heels completely in the nude. He could never walk in the shoes and he walked like a transvestite. He hadn't any visions of becoming a woman. He was happy as a man but cross-dressing was his buzz.

Basically all I had to do for him was to pose. He would put on music, pop music always with gay artists, and he would dance. It was a sort of jigging

120

with his cock flapping up to his belly. I would just lie on the bed on that clean white sheet wriggling in all sorts of poses: legs open, legs up there, always with high-heel shoes on. And he would go on dancing for about half an hour but he never spoke during the whole service. Not a word, but he would be looking at all the different pictures on his walls. Then he would come and stand over me and wank all over me but not over my face. He respected that. But wanking all over my body was his buzz.

During all this he would go out of the room a lot and I came to think that he was looking through a spy-hole at me. Sometimes he would pee on me. He would cover the floor with sheets in the bedroom or in the front room. He was definitely weird but he never ever frightened me.

Afterwards he would run me a bath and then he would start talking to me normally. That was it and I would go home. He was a kind man too. I had a very close friend who was also a working girl. If she was a bit skint I would ask Noel if she could come along too and he would always say yes and then he would pay double. She and I would do exactly the same thing, lying on the bed. He loved her because she wore high heels in general. I'll wear them for work but otherwise not.

As a client Noel went on for quite a few years but then I changed sauna and the bastard Max came into my life. That meant that I couldn't make arrangements or I had been beaten by Max and I wasn't going to turn up there with a black eye. It would have upset him. He knew there was something going on and that I wasn't the same girl. Since I had met Max the job for Noel felt different. I didn't look the same. I didn't sparkle the same. It fizzled out because I let him down quite a lot. I often think of him and I often pass his turning. I know he is still there because of the curtains but I would never knock.

Roy the wheelchair

Roy the Wheelchair was really quite a funny case. When he first rang the shop we knew he had a speech impediment. It was like he was talking through a voice-box on the phone. He kept ringing up and saying that he was disabled and he wanted to come in. He was in a wheelchair and do we have access? The girl I was working with and I kept saying, yes we do so come in, come in. He kept ringing up and ringing up and not coming in. Then one day the doorbell goes in the afternoon. The other girl goes to the

121

door and looks through the spy-hole. She comes running back laughing and saying, it's only him in the wheelchair. So we both go to the door and look through the spy-hole. We open up and there is this funny looking man sitting in the wheelchair. He looks like a chipmunk. He takes a look at us, says "Hello" and then he gets up out of the chair and walks in. My mate says "Fuck me, a miracle".

He walked in quite matter of fact and folded his chair as we looked at one another. Then he said "I have to do that to get my benefit". He put his wheelchair outside the room and went in.

Roy was in his sixties. He became a regular for quite a time. He wasn't a normal client at all. He liked to sit down with us for ages. He was overweight and he was a chain-smoker. He used to sit there in his fishnet tights and suspenders, shoes, socks and knickers. He wanted to sit there all day. We had to take it in turns to take him up to the end of the corridor, bend him over and give him six of the best. He really loved the cane. The harder the better. And at each stroke of the cane he would say "Yes miss" and "thank you miss". That went on all day. He would come at one o'clock and might still be there at five or six. He never got a hard-on when we caned him but then in the end he would go into the room and wank himself off. We didn't charge him a great deal because we didn't really have to do much for him apart from put up with having him sitting in there with us. Sometimes if he was getting our nerves with all that smoking we would make him go up to the end and stand in the corner with his hands on his head for half an hour.

Tom, the human toilet

"Is that you, Eliana? It's me, Tom", he would say on the 'phone. I'd reply in my usual chatty way but inside I didn't like it. I really didn't want to do what he wanted, but the money was good. He paid £250 ten years ago

"Are you coming in?" I'd ask in the usual way.

"Who are you with?" I'd say the name of the girl working with me.

"Will you both go to the toilet on me?"

"Of course", I'd say as this business is all about getting them through the door no matter what their buzz is. Once they are in you work it to your advantage. You are already halfway there. You have them interested.

Tom would lie down in the jacuzzi area with old towels underneath and you would stand above, legs wide open, and piss in his mouth. He would drink every drop, and if you could do some shit he would eat that too. His cock would be dead and he would have no desire for you to make him come. Just to be used as a human toilet was his buzz. That's what really turned him on. And he was not alone in that category.

Marcus, the masochist

Marion was the name used by Marcus. The door bell would go. I'd open it and there SHE was. Black stockings, silk undies, high heels. £200 would be put into my hand and the show begins. The guy was unbelievable. He would change from his office suit in the lobby into the glamour wear. He'd walk in carrying a doctor's case and talk incessantly. The next hour was to open your eyes to the ultimate. He wanted to shock you. He was completely fucked. He would inject himself with some anaesthetic and then start piercing needles about five inches long through his testicles. Blood would come out and he used to thrust his hips back and forth with about 10 different needles right the way through his balls. He would then bang on about how he used to fuck his daughter and all the kinky parties he went to. He showed me where he actually had his penis spit open by an ex-professional nurse as part of a sex act apparently. It's called banana split. His buzz was all about pain. He never had an orgasm.

This kind of parties consisting of heavy domination used to be illegal at the time though some court cases have thrown out prosecutions provided it could be shown that everything that happened was between consenting adults. Some of Marcus's stories were horrific and would do my head in for the rest of the day. If you weren't a working girl you would never believe that these people existed.

Stan the footman

Stan is a guy who likes to worship feet. He's a foot fetish man and he pays me £50 a foot. All I have to do is to lie there. He sucks all my toes and licks my feet for about 15 minutes each. I lie there thinking about what bills I've got to pay next. Then I finish him off with my mouth using a condom of course. I never do oral or sex without a condom.

Paranoid Pete, the council man

Paranoid Pete is a pain in the arse, a nuisance. He catches us every time because he doesn't come in a lot so he still manages to catch me and the other girls out. He comes to the door and you think, there's something about him...what is it? He comes in all normal, but as soon as you get him in the room he becomes jittery. Then he says: "This is what I want. You've got to pretend I'm the man from the council. Then he'll start talking until he'll say all of a sudden: "That's it, I've got to go. I can't do this, I'm going". So I say: "OK then, you go". He says: "Or shall I stay. What shall I do?" I say: "Stay. If you feel relaxed enough to stay, just stay."

This goes on for about 20 minutes. Every time he brings in with him a carrier bag with clothes he has just bought from Marks and Spencer or Primark or wherever: shirt, pants, socks, t-shirt and trousers. Men's clothes. Then he puts them on. So he spends £30 to £40 on those clothes every time. He puts them on and a moment later he changes his mind, he takes them off and leaves them behind. He says put them in the bin, which I do straight away.

He never wants massage or any sort of treatment. He never gets that far which is why you have to take the money off him up front. If you don't he won't pay you. So you get the money out of him first. Then he starts being edgy and asks you for his money back. So I say: "I can't give it you back. You've spent 20 minutes in here pissing me off and now you are asking for your money back." He does it every single time and he never gets it back. So overall he has spent about £100 and got nothing for it. He puzzles me. He does the same to every other girl. He's quietly spoken and might have had quite a nice upbringing, but he's odd looking and a bit creepy. If I saw him in a pub I wouldn't want to go anywhere near him.

The rapist (blindfold man)

I've had a couple "rapists" in my life. They are a bit creepy but harmless. We still have one who is a regular in the shop. He talks incessantly: not dirty things, just things. He's in his forties and lives with his mum and dad. He's very paranoid about that. "Got to get back...got to get back for tea". At home he spends all his time in his bedroom. His hobby is going all

124

round the streets photographing people and he's shown me some of the photographs: ordinary people wearing ordinary clothes and not kids or anything like that. He also goes into shops in London, heavy sex shops.

His buzz is that he wants to blindfold you and he wants to pretend he is hurting you. It can be scary and you have got to know someone to let him do it. He pins you down and he starts shouting at you but he will keep saying to you it's only an act. Normally I don't allow blindfolds but there are two other girls at the shop who have done him. He pays well: £150 or £200. We call him the rapist because that is what he wants to act out. It is scary when you are blindfolded, naked and you may be in the shop on your own. He ties your hands behind your back and your feet too. And he gags you.

He knows the layout, he knows you are on your own and as you lie there you question yourself, has he raped someone? Is he premeditating to rape someone? Is this your bad day? But you think of the £200 and you think it's not going to happen. But you also think if he did do anything to me, fuck me, I'd be found in here bound and gagged. I think that is quite heavy. That can fuck my head for the day and make me drink. When he's gone you keep thinking about it because you know the guy isn't quite right. But that's your job.

Jim, the creep

Jim the Creep is an odd character. We used to look through the spy-hole and say, "Oh not Jim the Creep, not him!" He's about 4' 6", about six stone and never been married. He's another one who is an obsessive talker. He talks all the way through the massage and the service. All the time you are wanking him off he spends the whole time talking and he never seems ready to come. But after several years I've mastered the way to make it happen. We talk about black cocks going into a white pussy and that's it. I've cracked it but only after five years.

Before, I could be in there wanking him for an hour or more. You are sweating and for a man of his age his cock is rock hard. And you think, for fuck's sake, this is hard work. We tried every trick in the book with Jim. We tried two girls this way, that way. But now we've cracked it, we let him have some time and then we tell him about black cocks in white pussies and we bring him off.

125

Coke man Terry, the millionaire

Terry is a millionaire, good looking and a nice guy. All the girls liked this client. He really has his life sussed. He used to come in bang on the charlie. He'd probably been on a two day bender. Whatever girl was there, he'd have her. Then when he'd been in the room a little while he'd say "Go and get your mate in" and out would come another £100. But you would have to get on the gear with him. He would pour out lines and lines of coke. The girls were OK about that. Whether they drink, do drugs, puff or whatever their beef is, I haven't met many girls that don't do coke. It's all part and parcel of the package.

Trouble is that because he was on coke you don't really get anywhere. He doesn't get a buzz from sex. Most of the time he would say: "Don't worry about it, girls, forget it" because he couldn't get his cock up. He would be happy to snort another line and watch us fuck about with each other's tits.

Patrick, the IRA man

I was working in a very well known sauna in London. You had to be quite somebody to get a shift in there. I got a shift from 6.00 pm to 1.a.m and I was lucky to get it. This was a sauna where the Page 3 girls used to come from. Well known Page 3 girls had worked there in the past. That little shift of just seven hours could pick me up from £500 to a grand. Compare that with the East End where your client was £50 for sex. It was amazing see the different breeding of the clientele. "£150, £200...no sweat, dear."

The best ones were the ones who turned up at the end. My favourite was one who was crazy enough to tell me that he was in the IRA. He never would trust any English man. He would never get in a taxi unless it was driven by an Indian or a Pakistani. When he was in London he would get a little Indian guy to drive him everywhere. The Indian would bring him to the sauna, drive off and come back for him. He would come in having had bottles of scotch. He was loud, brash and always slagging off the government. He would go into a fit about Margaret Thatcher and he would bring in tapes with IRA songs about her. But what a guy! I never ever left that room with less than £250. If you'd made your money, you would have made £500 or £600 up to one o'clock in the morning. But it was always worth staying another hour for Patrick, believe you me. I remember that one time he came in and he had twenty-two grand in a bag.

The fight promoter

A number of years ago a client came into the shop. A girl called Ronnie was working with me. She was also mixed race being part Chinese, and very pretty. The client looked at the two of us and asked if any other girls were working. We told him there weren't. "How would you like to earn £200 each? I want you to fight", he said. Our jaws dropped.

This was something new but Ronnie and I were both up for it. We were wearing our usual sexy underwear and high heels. We took the money off the client and went to the Jacuzzi area where we cleared back all the furniture. "Right," he said, "Get on with it".

We'd never done this before so we began by throwing out slaps to each other's arms and bodies. "Harder he said, "much harder". So we began to punch too. "Harder" he shouted. Then, in a funny sort of way we did begin to fight. "Come on, you bitch" I shouted and Ronnie grabbed my hair and it hurt me. Before we knew what was happening we were really fighting quite hard. I ripped her bra off and she got mine yanked down. Our punches and pinches and scratches now were going all over the place and our boobs were getting marked. Meanwhile the client was sitting there wanking himself off. When he had come we knew we'd done the service and the fight was over.

Ronnie and I actually had a lot of bruises and scratch marks to show for it and we had both surprised ourselves. It was the first and only time I'd done that. The client never came back. Maybe he'd found some other girls in another place. That was ages before the days of girls wrestling and boxing in public which happens a bit now. Actually some clients do like to wrestle with the working girl and some girls offer this service, particularly getting their legs locked round the client in different places including his face. I don't offer that. It's specialist and you need a bed to do it on. Sauna rooms with massage tables won't do.

Mr Christie

One of my golden rules is never trust any client. Never go out with them; never give them your number. If you do, that is when you fuck things up. This is a classic example.

About 15 years ago before I got sick with ME (which used to be called the

127

Yuppie disease) I was working at a place in East London. This particular client was one of my regulars. He was hard work. He never wanted sex but was into mild S&M. He liked to blindfold you. I never minded that in the sauna because the receptionist always used to sit on the desk and it was a very small place. He was never going to do anything to me because he wouldn't get away with it. He was a client of mine for months and months. He used to want a blow-job that would go on for ever and ever. I would be blindfolded and on my knees in front of him sucking him. He used to place his hands on top of my head and keep pushing it further down his cock until I would gag. It would take ages, half an hour or more, for him to come. He was just a complete control freak. I'd have lock-jaw at the end but he paid me £150.

This guy took a shine to me and came in every single week. I trusted him and I started seeing him outside. This is how it came about. I left that sauna as I got a bit sick. This was before the ME really kicked in. I told him I was leaving the sauna. I said I don't know what I'm going to be doing for a little while but I needed to have a bit of a break. I had just got over Max and everything. I said I don't know what I'm going to be doing for money but I'm going to give up the shift here. He offered to see me privately twice a week and give me £300. This was a fantastic deal. I could give up working the shift and still have that amount of money definite.

Twice a week he would come and pick me up from my house. He rented a flat just for me in Essex and took me there. He lived in Upton Park but he never took me to his place. Looking back it all sounds too good to be true. He would pick me up at half past five and go to the flat and I would give him the same service.

But he was a creepy guy. At the sauna we used to call him Mr Christie or Ten Rillington Place because he reminded us of that man. He was the image of Christie, he always wore black gloves and he always had a case. When he picked me up and we were driving to the flat, there would be silence. This freaked me and I'd be thinking what the fuck is he that quiet for? I'd say "Are you all right, Billy?" and he'd take in a big deep breath and just say "Yes".

I'd known him first at a sauna where I was working in Southend. It was a lovely place. Lisa and I used to do the Saturday shift there. We loved it. We could do what we wanted. The boss used to leave us alone. We used the day to do all our beauty treatments and generally have a laugh because it was that quiet. We'd do a couple of clients if we were lucky.

Christie started coming in there. He was an all-right client but you never got out of the room in less than an hour. One day he comes in and I go up to the room with him. We spend an hour there and his service is finished but his glasses fell on the floor. I accidentally trod on them and I saw him turn. I hadn't broken the glasses, just bent the arm. I said "Oh, I'm so sorry". I saw his face turn, for whatever reason I don't know. I couldn't believe I had upset him that much. He went "For fuck's sake". I felt that's not like him and I was scared. I apologised: "I am so sorry. It was an accident. I didn't realise your glasses were on the floor." It worried me and it puzzled me that I had upset him that much. He went off in a huff. He flew down the stairs, flew out of the door. Lisa asked "What the fuck has gone on?" I told her what had happened and she said "I told you he was creepy".

We left by the back entrance as we always did and he used to do that too. I got into my car as we were going back to Lisa's place. It was a ritual. We always used to go to her and get pissed. My mum used to babysit for me so she knew I wasn't coming home on Saturdays.

I was driving along and looked in my mirror and I thought "mmm", those headlights are a bit close. I said to Lisa, "do you see that car behind? I know who's in there and he is following us. It's fucking Christie". I couldn't see him but I just knew.

This is near Southend and we are going to Wanstead which is over an hour away. As I knew all about his blind-folding I felt like shitting myself. He had gone on the turn because I had stepped on his glasses. What the fuck is he doing? Why is he following me?

After a bit we get to a narrow lane. It's a winding country road and if you don't know that road you are going to end up in a ditch. I know that road like the back of my hand. You do twenty down that road but I can do fifty because I know where every bend is. As soon as I hit the lane we were approaching where Lisa lives and he is still behind me. So I put my foot down and I said "Lisa, I've got to do this. We've got to lose him. We can't bring him to your door. If need be I'll go to the police station because we can't have him following me." She just said "Be careful".

I could see he was struggling to keep with us and he meant business. What was he going to do, kill us? What's he doing? He's followed us from the sauna?

He struggled to keep up and then he caught us at some traffic lights.

Lisa's partner is a big black guy, a doorman built like a brick shit-house. You don't mess with him. Lisa got out her mobile and rang him. "We are going to be pulling up in a minute. We have Christie the Creep from the sauna. He's followed us all the way from Southend. Help us. When we pull up we are going to get out."

We pull up outside Lisa's house and this giant of a guy comes out. I get out. Lisa gets out. Christie the Creep has pulled up three cars behind. What's he going to do now? Lisa's guy has come to the gate. He's got a baseball bat and Christie can't see it because it's behind his back. He says "what's going on?" I said "Nothing. I ain't done nothing. Ain't ripped him off or anything. He's a client of mine. I just stepped on his glasses and he's followed us all the way home."

Lisa's guy goes up to Christie's car with the baseball bat behind him. He taps on the window and says "Pull your window down". Christie can't see the baseball bat. He pulls the window down and the baseball bat goes CRACK on his windscreen. He wasn't expecting that! Lisa's partner has cracked his windscreen and bashed his bonnet and now he is trying to get Christie out of the car. He shouts "You just followed my missus home, you fucker. Now fuck off". Christie went off like a shot. I guess Christie was the lucky one at the end of that day. After that he disappeared off the scene and I never saw him again until he turned up at a sauna in the City three years later.

On the day he walked into the sauna in the City I thought "Fuck, he's found me" I thought, fucking hell, he's going come to settle with me for the baseball bat episode but he never mentioned it and neither did I. I didn't ask him how he had found me either because I didn't want to go back over the previous episode.

He became a client there at the sauna for two years until I decided to leave. During that time he wanted the same things and I gave him the service which was a form of mild submission. When I told him I was going he said

130

"I will be your private client and keep you going until you decide what you are going to do. Looking back I was stupid to trust him and I should have known better but the offer was such a good one.

For a couple of months it was OK. He would pick me up and we would go to the flat. He would do the usual things. Once we got to the flat he would go into silent mode. His ritual would be to do the blindfold, tie my hands behind my back and have me kneel. He would never take his clothes off. He'd put a condom on and then his cock would go in my mouth. I was nervous. In the sauna it was fine, but for £300 a week I took the risk.

Sucking him off would go on and on and on. It seemed like eternity. Just my head going back and forwards and not being able to use my fingers on him at all. He was difficult to make come because he had that self-control. He was a control freak. He would come when he wanted. My eyes would be tight shut while I was doing it even though they were behind the blindfold. He would be silent, deadly silent. Not a murmur, not even when he came.

Even though he had a condom and was dead silent I knew when he had come. That's something I mastered ages ago. I've been tricked too many times by guys wanting me to keep on sucking after they've come. Some guys stay up even after they have come and they want me to go on sucking them. For me when a guy comes that's it. He doesn't get a second helping unless he pays for it. They would tell me that they hadn't come and they would want me to keep on sucking or fucking but you learn to know when they come.

The long spells of silence in the car with Christie would give me the creeps. I would speak to him and he wouldn't answer me. I would feel nervous all the way to the flat and even on the way back. I would tell my friend every time I was going to see Christie and I would ring her when I left. I told her, if you don't hear from me call the police.

I always felt that he was planning to do something to me because when we got to the flat he used to wear the gloves. Black leather. I didn't like it. His silences were getting more and he was making me nervous. But he had got me relying on his £300 a week in my cushy little life. I didn't have to go to the sauna any more. My rent was being paid by the housing benefit. I got complacent with that.

131

Christie got weirder. The silences got longer and he had this habit of standing there and drawing his breath in and clenching his fists. I would ask: "Are you all right?" and he wouldn't go "Yes, I'm OK". He would just let his sigh out and look at me, while I was thinking what a fucking nutter you are.

Christie started getting very controlling towards me. He would ring me up during the day. If I didn't answer him he would turn up at my house. He had got me.

One day he took me to his flat as usual and I walked in. He had obviously been there in advance. There was a stool. On it was a hammer, a screwdriver and a piece of rope. Straight away I clocked the stool in the corner. All placed neatly there. Hammer, screwdriver, rope. I felt very uneasy.

In the car there had been no speaking. In the flat I knelt down in front of him as usual and I put the blindfold on but something in my stomach was telling me it was wrong. I am putting the blindfold on myself and do it very loose. I feel sick. I'm shaking. I don't feel right. I can't do this with this guy anymore. I feel him take step back towards the stool which was right behind him. I thought there are two things here. Either you are going to do me in or it's part of your buzz to freak me out but I'm the wrong girl for you. I knew he had taken a step back and I felt he was going to touch something on the stool. I rip off my blindfold off and he is standing there and his hand is about to take one of those items off the stool.

I run out of the flat screaming down the balcony, phoning my friend. I run into the cul-de-sac and hide behind a bush. He comes down with a torch and is shining it all around. On the phone Lisa says stay exactly where you are. We're coming to get you. And she and her boyfriend came. There I am hiding behind a bush wearing my sexy clothes and shivering with terror. She knew the address and the layout there and exactly where I was.

I've always thought Christie was planning something that night. He never contacted me afterwards. He disappeared and I never saw him again.

Chapter 15
DRUGS, HEALTH AND PERSONAL SAFETY

Security

As I advertise the sauna a lot in local shop windows and we have a sign saying "Sauna and massage" above the door obviously anybody can walk in off the street. I have to think about the security of me and the girls. We have a spy-hole, a chain across the door, a CCTV and we have a guy who sits there in the shop. He is a lonely little guy who gets through beer but he looks after the shop and the girls. I'm lucky to have that sort of man around. He's not a bouncer but he's there and he has a mobile so you know that if you shouted for help he'd be on his mobile to the police. So there's always a presence at my shop.

I found him by word of mouth. It's not a job you can advertise in the job centre. I don't pay him a wage in the normal sense because he's on social security anyway, but he gets his beers and cigarettes and it's a friendly place to be. Sometimes he sleeps on the premises. You might think it a bit hard for him to be in a place with girls wearing sexy clothes, with bras and panties visible and fucking happening in the rooms all the day, but he just got used to that. It's his job like it is ours. He doesn't ask us for sex. He's like part of the family. He's seen it all before.

He helps run the place by opening the place up, vacuuming it, cleaning the showers and turning on the heating. One really important thing he does is getting cards about the sauna put up in newsagents' notice boards and doing the shopping. Also he answers the phone if the girls are busy. It's not ideal having a man answering the phone because clients want to hear a girl's voice and to find out who is working that day. A lot of callers just put the phone down when they hear a man's voice but that can't be helped. But if the caller is one of our partners it is useful because he can pass the message.

I've worked in lots of different saunas but there was only one which had a doorman for security. It was a place that was open late, had a lot of girls and plenty of cash turnover. That was for a well known madam. It was

133

worth her paying £100 for security to stand there for a few hours.

When saunas were doing well they had a receptionist to answer the phone. These days most saunas have the girls do that themselves. The boss has to be careful and to know the receptionist very well because she is the key link. If the girls can sweeten up the receptionist they can fuck your business. She's got to be completely loyal to her boss. Also, your business has to be turning over a decent amount on a daily basis to be able to afford one. A receptionist may be a former working girl. In a flat there is usually a maid who meets clients as they ring the bell and tells them about the girl if she is busy at the time. The receptionist and the maid generally tell the client what the girls will do.

I've always felt secure in saunas even in a small one like mine that doesn't have a receptionist. Sometimes though I do open the door to a guy who says "Oh, are you on your own? " Of course you never let the client know you are on your own. When they come in that is where the massage rooms are. They don't walk along the corridor to the room where the girls sit so they don't know if you are on your own. They don't go there unless you invite them and very few clients get invited. They are the exceptions like Roy, the wheelchair man.

Another exception is one of my regulars who has been coming to the sauna for a couple of years. We've got to know him and we all like him. He comes into our room and brings a bottle of wine or some cans of beer. He chats in the girls' room about whatever is going on his life like the films he has been to or what he has done over the weekend. He's well spoken and sometimes brings us little presents like stockings or a potted plant. Once in a while he'll get us some burgers or chips when we are hungry. After a bit he says to me, let's go to the room and we do the things he likes which by now I know really well. Afterwards he comes back into the girls' room in a matter of fact way as though he had just been out for a pee and he chats a bit more before he goes.

He is someone who we all accept because he is a very regular client. He doesn't seem at all the lonely type and he tells us about some of the things he does. I should say he has plenty of interests but I think he finds our lifestyle so different from whatever he has grown up with that just being in the girls' room gives him a buzz. In the massage room itself he likes plenty of variety including a bit of dressing up but nothing really out of the

134

ordinary. The other girls like having him there because he is a break from watching TV. At Christmas he brings in cards, mince pies and mulled wine to heat up in the microwave.

Drugs

I've done coke all my life but I have never been addicted. I hardly ever do it now but I still enjoy a joint now and then. The real addicts are the girls on the streets you read about in the papers but I have also known some sauna girls who were addicts. The minute they had done a client they were on the phone to their dealer. I call it "clucking" which means that they were desperate for their next fix. I don't have that in my shop because I don't have girls with drugs problems.

I'm lucky not to have become addicted to coke. The reason is because I am a girl that likes expensive things. This may seem a bit odd but for me there is no way that I am going to spend £100 on coke when I would rather spend it on an expensive cushion. My buzz would be the cushion so if it was between the two, the cushion would win. My coke was always supplied to me by the people I hung around with, so if it was free and ready I'd do it. When you are with wide boys who have got thousands to spend it's no problem to snort hundreds of pounds of Charlie in one night because it is readily available and free.

Snorting that amount of cocaine would make me high as a kite. I would be up all night, and the next morning I would be feeling like shit and trying to get down. It would put me out of the game for a day.

Health

I'm self-employed so when I don't work I don't earn. I can't afford sickies and away days and I have to be in the shop at least twice a week to see regular clients, go to the bank, pay bills and do the things that the boss of any small business has to do. I'm lucky. My health has generally been good. I'm not one of those people who run and whinge to the doctor for every spot and ache and pain anyway. I have had this conversation many times with friends and with my partner. What I have drunk and put in my body over the years, another person would probably be dead. I've done alcohol abuse, drug abuse and cigarette abuse. I don't know whether it has done any lasting damage but I've got a strong constitution.

135

I'm making an effort to clean myself up. Not long back I decided to give up alcohol, just like that. That was surprising and sudden but not at all hard. I didn't taper off, I just stopped. I drink a lot of cranberry juice now and that's good for you anyway. Cutting down the ciggies is proving much harder. I used to do 30 or so a day including a lot of rollies which I roll myself. I saw an advertisement for electronic cigarettes and a friend gave me a kit for Christmas. They've helped quite a lot. They work on the craving and they give you something to do with your fingers because they are like cigarettes. You puff on them and get a form of vapour in your mouth. I'm down to about 10 real cigs a day now and I really want to kick the habit altogether.

As for sexually transmitted diseases, for me the condom has always been the golden rule. If you do things for one client without a condom you are going to do it again. If a client offers you £100 say to do oral without a condom, you do it once and he'll want it again. Doing sex without condoms is very risky. It's as simple as that.

Sometimes I have been worried when there has been an accident because the client has burst a condom. That's when you panic, that's when fear kicks in. It fucks your head up. You ask any working girl. You feel awful. You feel dirty. It's a horrible horrible feeling. You go home. You feel dirty towards your partner, you feel horrible to yourself. That's when girls go running to the clinic for the morning-after pill. They say they've had a burst condom and can they get checked over. It's a worry but it leaves you after a few days if you stop thinking about it.

One of my footballer clients deliberately burst a condom with me which doesn't happen often. It's happened to me only ten or so times in my 20 years. The footballer did it by tearing it open when he was having sex with me. I've had regular smear tests and they will tell you straight away if you have got anything.

Health worries are the reason why a lot of working girls are reluctant to kiss. A lot of clients ask them do they kiss. For many it is a personal no-no. Also kissing is intimate. Kissing is what you do with your partner. So if you go full swing sticking your tongue down every client's throat, how do you know what you are going to catch? How do you know that the man hasn't got Aids or a cut in his mouth? And how does he know that you haven't either? The same applies if he is willing to fuck you without a condom, how does he know about you? I could be doing that with every man who comes through the door. Why would you want to take the risk? Why would you want to be doing that with me? It doesn't make sense. If I was a man I wouldn't want to fuck a girl in a sauna without a condom.

Though I'm fit and healthy now I went through a bad two years when I couldn't work at all. I contracted ME that used to be called the yuppies' disease. I couldn't even get out of bed. My mum moved in and cared for me and the children. During the period sometimes I would be lying there and I would wake up and see myself on the other side of the room. I felt like someone had pulled me out of bed and put me back into bed again. I used to wake up and look round the room and think I am over on the other side. To this day I don't know if I was just sick or if something was flying me round the room. It happened a few times.

For two years I had been lying in bed with ME. I could only just about get out of bed to go slowly to the toilet. Everything I did took me ages and to make a cup of tea was like asking me to walk to the end of the world. In the morning I couldn't do it because my energy was very low. By the afternoon it would be a little better. I would sit in the kitchen for ten minutes and then I would think I really had to get back to bed.

One day my mum came in. She had just got back from school and she burst the door open. She said: "Right, get up. You can't keep lying in your bed. You've got to get up. Your cuppa is in the kitchen. Today you are getting up". It was the way she said it that hit me. My mum is such a gentle woman but she had switched. And when she switches, she switches. She left the room and I heard her shouting:" You're going to have to get up because I'm not going to bring up your kids. This is enough. You are going to have to get up".

She made me get up. She refused to bring my tea. She refused to do anything and she said she wanted to go home. She said it was about time I got myself out of the bed because there was no cure for me. "You're going to have to help yourself".

And that was it. I got out of bed and got to the kitchen. I picked up the cup of tea and she said "You're not going back into that bedroom today." She'd done it. She broke it. From then on slowly I began to pick up. It was a mind thing. My ME was brought on by stress, my lifestyle and the shit I

137

had been through. Drugs, drink: I was completely burned out physically and mentally. After that I went to a self-help group in Billericay and my mum did everything for me as I built up strength.

From the day my mum told me to get out of bed to the day I started off again as a working girl took a few months. I began with one shift a week, eleven till eleven. That was enough for me for a long time. I was all right financially. I was drawing benefit and one day at the sauna gave me £200-£300 a week. I was all right and life was much better.

Outreach workers

Some health authorities used to employ outreach workers. They were nurses who would come and see us now and then to tell us about sexual health. They were very helpful and they used to supply condoms and KY jelly. If any girl had something wrong downstairs they would be there with the tablets and the creams. We had an outreach worker called Mary who came to see us for years. She was very good, very helpful. You could ring her at any time, morning, noon or night. She would get the drugs or the supplies to you there and then or do it after work. With the cuts in the health budgets we no longer have outreach workers coming to visit us. If we want to see a nurse we have to go to the sexual health clinic in the hospital.

Mary and the other outreach workers never tried to get us to leave the game. They were professional nurses and recognized that we are professional working girls. We were their job. If we weren't there they wouldn't have had a job. Sometimes we have Bible-bashers at the door. I'm very polite to them because they are really nice to us. I don't let them in but I know girls who have. I just greet them at the door and take their leaflet. They are polite to us and don't try to force themselves on us. Then I wish them good-day. They obviously know what we do but they've never tried to take us off the game. That has never happened to me in 20 years.

Sexual health clinics provide free condoms still. Mary used to bring them for us by the hundreds in boxes and boxes. Maybe that put the kybosh on the system. If you go to the clinic and are brazen enough to say you are a working girl they'll give you twice as much as normal.

Condoms vary a bit in thickness and size. The ones Mary brought were tough and so they were good for us working girls. There are all sorts of condoms on the market now. We like to use flavoured ones for giving French. Ordinary condoms have a lubricant and that's not much good for you because you are swallowing chemicals. Years ago they had Amoxyl on them which was supposed to kill the Aids virus but it tasted disgusting. That's when I started using the flavoured ones.

In theory we don't have condoms in the shop. But clients don't bring them so we keep them in our handbags or hidden in locked drawers where we keep our personal things. We say the sizes they come in are small, medium and liar! If you get a guy who is extra small and you put a standard condom on it is flopping about. The worst thing is if you are doing French and the condom gets stuck down the back of your tonsils. And if you are doing sex and the guy is small, it may come off inside you and that is a big risk.

Then you get the guy who is really big and the condom only fits on halfway and that can be dangerous too. A normal guy is six inches when he's hard but you get some guys who are much bigger. Even up to nine inches, I'd say. They aren't necessarily black. We see rather more black men now than we used to but saunas aren't really a black man's thing. They had a reputation for being more on the pimping end of it and also for robbing us. A lot of girls wouldn't let them in for that reason so sometimes we get callers who say "I'm black, does that matter?" Black men think they should always get sex for nothing. They've got pussy everywhere, black pussy, white pussy. Why pay for it?

If the guy is really big and wants to take you from behind that can hurt a bit as his cock hits the inside wall of your pussy. Some big guys know they are big, and they are gentle. Other ones couldn't give a fuck because they know what they are going to do when you bend over. Also when you bend over some clients try to get in your bum. I put my hand down and push the cock away or else I just say "Please don't touch me there. I don't like it". I'd say that out of ten clients, two will ask for anal. Some girls don't mind giving it and they all charge extra. It needs to be agreed right up front.

When you find you've got a client with a big cock you know you can cope with him as hand-relief but you can guarantee he is going to want French and sex. When you're doing French he'll tell you to go down further and you can't. The condom only covers half the cock, and then they want sex. If he's not gentle with you he can hurt you. As he is banging away you are

139

getting dryer and dryer and the condom is getting weaker and weaker. That's when it becomes dangerous and the condom can burst. We are talking of men with nine inch cocks and lots of width as well. You can't tell just from the height of the man. I've seen men over six feet tall with two inch willies.

Chapter 16
MONEY

Cash and the taxman

The day-to-day running of a sauna is all in cash. In the old days of saunas in the City yuppies would sometimes pay with a cheque and sometimes it would bounce. Some of the girls would put a squeeze on the client by getting in touch with the bank and saying who they were and the services that the cheque had been given for. This didn't happen much and never happens today. Why should any client want to lay himself open to how he is spending the house-keeping?

We ask clients for their first names and this is so that I know how much money to collect off the girls. We keep the names for the accountant to work with. I tear the sheet for the day off the pad and bung into an envelope. The accountant has to spend the first few evenings sorting them out. I am much more methodical with the bills I pay such as phone, heating, water, council tax, repairs and petrol. I try to keep something in reserve for when the tax demand comes in but it is hard and it's a day I dread. I don't want to be done by the Revenue like some of the bosses I have worked for. Actually there has been very little profit in saunas since the recession. The last couple of years have been dreadful and I know of several saunas that have closed down.

When I retire I shall draw a state pension in the usual way because I have paid my national insurance contributions as a self-employed girl.

I have an accountant who I took over from my previous partner and I just keep using him. It's easier that way as he knows how to work my books. If he does a good job I'll not have to pay much. He knows that I hate getting anything in the post from the Revenue. He tells me, if you get anything from them at the shop or at your house, don't open it. There's no need to give yourself grief. Just give it to me. If the Revenue dumps a bill on me I can't manage, I just tell them that I haven't got the money and I do a deal to pay off something every month. I pay very little tax because business is so bad. We are all praying that when the recession is over business will pick up again. I've never had to struggle like this before to keep the sauna's door

141

open.

Becoming a business owner

The sauna business is pretty much like other small businesses outside. Someone has to own it, run it, manage the people who work for you — and that isn't just the girls — pay the bills, see to the repairs and deal with the council and the taxman. Then there are the day-to-day crises when a girl goes off sick or gets threatened by a client who is drunk, or on crack, or abusive or all of them. A lot of the things that have to be done to keep the shop's door open aren't noticed by the girls themselves so it is inevitable that some of them think it would be much better to be the sauna's owner or boss and make a mint from the shift money that they pay. In the good times up to the past five years they may have been right, but things were turning down for saunas even before the recession began.

In my case, 15 years ago I actually worked one shift a week in the place that I run now. At the time I was working in other saunas in and around London. Through word of mouth I got this shift. It was a Friday shift and a busy shift so I was quite lucky. It was a nice cosy little place, not clinical like the other places that had invested lots of money in wooden floors. This was more an old-fashioned sort of place. One thing that was different was that the girls were older, typically in their 30s and 40s whereas the girls in the other places I worked were much younger.

It was comfortable and run very simply. The boss was a lovely bubbly little lady, Lizzie, who had been a working girl herself. I stayed there for about a year and went on to work at other places. After some time, now that I had a car and could get round more, I gave Lizzie a ring to see if she had a shift. Much to my surprise it turned out that I had rung her at just the right time because she had three, so I went back there and did three shifts a week. I got very friendly with her. We got on like a house on fire and became very good friends, which we still are. The place was ticking over, not buzzing, just ticking over. She was 20 years older than me and was going through a divorce. I could see the place's potential. She was still working shifts herself and a lot of the time we were on the same shifts together. I would say to her, "You shouldn't be here working for this place. This place should be working for you".

I could see that the place needed an injection to liven it up but she had got despondent. So gradually I tried to build up her confidence so that she could turn things around. She needed to put the door money up a bit and get some new girls so we started to get the business going. Then she asked me if I would be interested in a partnership with her. Straight away I said yes, and from there our little place took off. We got a loan of £7,000 and refurbished the place. I had an excellent builder who I had known for years. He came and gutted the place and had it up and running for us in three weeks. We had adverts out in newspapers everywhere and it worked. We had turned it around. That was how I first got into becoming a boss, though not a madam, because I was still working shifts as well, like I do today.

Lizzie was a loyal and totally trustworthy in friendship and partnership. She had a terrific sense of humour and if you travelled the world over you wouldn't find anyone to match her. She was her own boss who gave me the chance to be mine and still is a great friend to this day.

Lizzie was having complications in her private life and wanted to leave so I took over. As a result of her divorce she had a house and some money in the bank. She also fell in love with another guy and it was the way out for her. I always say she got out at the right time.

When I took over the business I inherited her right hand man. He was called Arthur and had been with the business even before Lizzie. He didn't have a financial stake in the business but he opened up the shop each day and closed it, looked out for the girls, did the shopping and we were his life. He was very kind to all of us, me in particular. He was an alcoholic but never a nasty drunk. He never made passes at any of the girls, still less try to take advantage of them. When I was going through bad times I would talk with him for hours and sometimes spend the night at his place though never sexually. He was a wonderful friend and really cared about us.

When I took over the place it included being responsible for paying back the loan. I gave Lizzie a bit of goodwill money because she had previously given that amount to go in with the person before. And that was it. I didn't own the premises but I owned the business. There was nothing in writing and the money was exchanged in a brown paper bag. So there I was, the manager of a small sauna business. I took on the responsibility of keeping it going, in particular of paying the rent to the landlord. He knows what goes on and providing the rent is paid on time he stays away. He is responsible for big things like roof repairs and the water and heating system. It's hard

143

to get them done but he does it after a bit if I nag him. He never visits the sauna unless he really has to. He never comes as a client. It is a completely professional relationship.

Being a sauna boss is like running any other small business which sells a service. It relies on the goodwill of the girls who work there and the clients who come. All this represents the value of the business should I want to sell it and I think about that every single day. I'm quite lucky where I am really. I have no lease so I can walk away. I have only got to give the landlord three months notice and I can be gone. I could pass the goodwill down to somebody and hope to make myself a little bit of money in a brown paper bag. All I am selling is the goodwill and the phone number. I think that the phone number is worth a grand and I could sell it to a flat or to another sauna and they would get my clients. If I wanted out I would have to speak to the landlord and tell him he can trust this girl to take over from me. He doesn't care about money in a brown bag. All he cares about is his rent being paid. If I wanted to stop at any time I could simply close the door. There is nothing in writing. He could give me notice too and could call the property back at any time. That's why I'm always punctual with the rent however much I am struggling. The furniture and other things in the place aren't worth much to anyone.

I know I'm OK at the moment because he is in property and has a lot of headaches so he wouldn't want to see me go. He's getting regular rent from the sauna, so he's OK.

As for the girls who work for me, they would carry on as working girls elsewhere. Some of them work elsewhere anyway but getting additional shifts isn't easy these days. Saunas' best days have gone. Clients will always want the services provided by working girls but they have less money to spend and are wanting the same service for less money. I've often thought that saunas are a dying business.

Chapter 17
CHANGES IN THE LAW FOR WORKING GIRLS?

Legalise brothels or ban them?

Running a sauna has always been a grey part of the law. They aren't brothels really because some clients come in and genuinely want just a sauna and a massage. In theory nobody knows what goes on inside the room afterwards though it is an open secret what we do. Paying for sex isn't illegal but touting and soliciting always have been. Street girls used to get picked up for touting and given a fine in the magistrates' court the next day. The fines weren't enough to stop them going on the street again straight away which they probably had to do to pay the fine anyway.

Taking money off a working girl is the tricky bit because if the police do a raid they want to get at the boss or the madam who mostly isn't around. I work like the other girls in my shop and if a client asks who the boss is we keep our mouths shut. The idea that a new law should fine clients and not the girls or the shop is a funny one. You can have any moral view you like about whether men should pay for sex but the fact is that working girls provide a service like other professions. Lawyers charge by the hour and you pay for their time. Gardeners and other manual workers too. You don't have to use them. The same goes with us. You can do it yourself as a lawyer or a gardener if you want to, and you can do it yourself as a man by wanking off. All men masturbate from an early age but working girls give more pleasure and in plenty of cases they enable clients to fulfil fantasies. Also we are all good-looking. Some of us are really stunning so men get pleasure that can be looked on as a treat. When the treat is finished both sides feel satisfied. Both have got what they wanted in a simple and matter of fact way.

Fining clients?

Fining clients seems to be an idea imported from Scandinavia. I think that for a long time Scandinavian women were much freer with sex than in this country so maybe there didn't need to be so many working girls. If the police started raiding saunas and fining any clients who happened to be there at the time I think it would hit us hard. Men don't want their partners to know what they are up to. The woman must feel hurt and rejected unless she has boyfriends on the side too. Women enjoy sex but they aren't as sexually driven as men. If men had less sex drive working girls would be out of a job.

What we do is called the oldest profession. Like me, most girls have chosen it freely as a way of earning more money than anything else we could do. No training is necessary: just a nice body and face and a nice personality and boom-boom you've got a job which will see you through a lot of years. There is plenty of down-side too which this book tells you about. The main one is putting you on the wrong side of the fence in relationships with the rest of the world. You don't think much about that to begin with because the money is so good.

I've sometimes wondered what I would do if saunas were classified as brothels and had to be licensed. I think that is what happens in Australia. My initial reaction would be "Oh God, I can't be dealing with that. I'll close the door". I don't know if I would want to go through registration with the council or whether the other girls would want to work in a registered place. Things seem to work OK as they are so I just hope that politicians don't try to get in on the act and make things difficult for us. If saunas disappeared our clients would look for girls working in flats so it wouldn't make any difference. You could say that it was just being driven underground.

How working girls save clients' conventional relationships

If you want our side of the argument you can say that for some clients coming to a sauna is actually good for their family life. We get clients who tell us that they have been married or in a relationship for a long time and still love the partner and the kids, but they don't get any buzz from sex with their partners. Some say the partner has gone off sex and what she doesn't know doesn't hurt. The papers have agony columns about infidelity and the marriage guidance people are supposed to give sex advice too. All that sort of thing including going to counselling as a couple takes time and money and at the end of the day coming to us is such a simple solution. The man gets satisfaction and doesn't break up the family by walking off with a new partner.

The latest way of describing what we do is "the girlfriend experience". Guys who have plenty of money can get an escort for an evening and even an overnight stay. He knows they will end up in bed and maybe he'll get a few fantasies fulfilled as well but it will cost him £150 upwards. We provide a lot of what he wants including really good sex for £50 upwards so he gets an awful lot more fun for his money.

When men say their partner has gone off sex I can believe that. Some are quite nice guys and if that is just the missing bit in their relationship then the service we provide can be looked on a helpful. A few men even say to us "I think she probably knows".

If men are still good providers and are good dads the sex thing they get from us seems a good solution. A man can still be a good person and the other bits of the relationship aren't affected. I've known just a few clients who come to me and who make me get them hard and excited but say "Don't make me come. Don't make me come". They want to get revved up so that they can go home and give it to their missus. That is really an exception because not many guys can get close to coming and not let it happen, but if the partner gets the benefit of sex that's good for both of them. Really we are quite useful, aren't we!

Chapter 18
FOREIGN GIRLS AND TRAFFICKING

Whenever there is a story in the papers about foreign girls in saunas it is bad for us. Some of it is obviously true and the girls have been tricked to come here from the poor parts of the EU. They've been told they'll get jobs as models or something and find themselves working in saunas. They have big debts to the traffickers for getting them here and as the traffickers are part of the criminal gangs in their own countries the families at home are threatened. Very likely the traffickers have taken away their passports. The law is right to raid those places and give the girls safe refuge. Personally I am reluctant to take on foreign girls though I have taken on some in the past, though not in the last couple of years. The ones on offer used to be Brazilians and Thai girls. Now it is more Albanians. I did take on a couple of Albanian girls but it was nothing but aggravation. It starts OK. A girl comes to the shop and asks for a shift. She is stunningly beautiful and speaks good English so you think I'll have her. Before long her friend comes along and you think, I must have her too. But it soon becomes apparent they've got a man behind them because their phones don't stop ringing. The next thing is that I get phone calls from the pimps themselves saying they want to put more girls into the shop. You can see that they really want to take it over.

Another thing is that the girls they send are younger than my girls. I think it is a fallacy that every man wants a young girl. I have taken on some lovely young girls but the client sees them once and doesn't want them again. This is because they are hard, they are under pressure, they don't smile and maybe they don't want to be fucked in the room at all. They don't have the English dialect, they don't work the way English working girls do. Some clients have said "beautiful girl, but she doesn't smile". That's no good. The client doesn't want her. He'd rather have a girl who is 20 years older, gives him a nice massage, cares for him, looks after him and makes it all seem fun. I said to these Albanian girls, you are beautiful but you don't smile. You've got to smile at the clients. You've got to make the client feel welcome the moment you open the door for him and say come in! Albanian girls just don't get it.

Chapter 19
THE CHANGING FACE OF THE BUSINESS

Alongside the recession which has hit saunas hard is the Internet. Girls advertising themselves used to be done by putting cards up in phone boxes. That's illegal now. The Internet is a godsend for girls working from flats. They can get someone to make a website for them including very explicit photos. They don't need to advertise in the local papers and the papers are getting harder about taking these ads anyway. They don't need to put up cards in newsagents. They can join Punternet with photos, very detailed statements and a tick-box form showing the services they do and don't offer. They can have a mobile phone as their business number and a separate mobile for the other part of their lives. It's all that easy.

Even ten years ago we sauna girls used to moan about girls working from flats which were not in the abundance they are today. When you were in a sauna you always knew when a flat had opened up because the sauna would go quiet. You'd get the local paper and look for the heading "New girl". You'd ring up and find it was three turnings away and that is why the shop is quiet. Flats used to come and go and they have always been a problem to the saunas. Now they are around to stay.

Girls who work from flats generally live there too. That's a big disadvantage because it makes it hard to keep the two lives apart the way we can do when we work in saunas. In the earlier days you went and got a flat with another girl, you paid the deposit, you worked from the flat Monday to Friday or you stuck someone else in there and then you went home. Now it is quite common for a girl to work from the flat she lives in. Some flats are owned by a boss who organises the girls to work there on a rota.

The advertising on Punternet is very detailed. Most of the photos are full face, full body and always with a description of what the girls will do. Another thing is the field reports sent in by punters about their experience with individual girls. These reports are very explicit beginning with how long the visit lasted and what it cost. After that comes detail about what the girl did for the money and finishing up with two simple questions: 1) would

151

the punter recommend the girl? and 2) would he go to her again?

Some girls get a lot of field reports and clearly this is a good form of advertising. Nearly all the reports are favourable and the system has a safety valve to allow the girl to correct things which she feels are wrong in a report. It is a powerful site which has helped the flats a lot and the girls who work there. Saunas get listed too. In my shop we don't want to have our faces and bodies up there in lights on the Internet. My business is much more discreet.

The girlfriend experience

On Punternet and elsewhere you read about a new development among working girls. It seems to have become established quite quickly and it is known as 'the girlfriend experience', shortened to GFE. The difference is that the girl agrees an amount of time with the client and doesn't just get him to orgasm as soon as possible and stop things there. So the guy expects to chat a bit, have a drink together and then do things that a real girlfriend would do like deep kissing and maybe oral without a condom though not necessarily to completion. Clearly these things have to be agreed and the girl will have her boundaries. But the concept is that while the client is with the girl she behaves more like a girlfriend than a working girl.

In my shop we don't go down that route which we call 'heavy'. I wouldn't employ a 'heavy' girl in my sauna. If I had a flat and I put girls in I might use heavy girls. I couldn't bring a girl like that to the sauna because it would wreck the business for the other girls. The girls in my sauna are professional girls. They find out what the client wants and they give it to him. When he has come, he's been done, finished, whatever the clock says.

And what are these GFE girls letting themselves in for? If they do three or four guys a day with deep kissing, they don't know what those guys have in their mouths. They could have herpes, they could have Aids, they could have anything. What kind of girls want to put their lives at risk for whatever money I just don't know. Just add it up. Three guys a day for three days a week, that's going on 40 guys in a month and you are letting them put their tongues down the back of your throat. You don't know what they've got and they don't know what you've got. For me it's a no-no, and that's just one more reason why I want to get out of the business. It's becoming harder, heavier, and you can't compete with girls who will do

152

GFE. Yes they charge a lot more, starting at about £100 but men are fickle. If they want to stick their tongues down your throat and you aren't going to do it, it doesn't matter how beautiful you are, they'll go off and find a girl who will do it. I don't want a man coming in and putting his tongue down my throat when he has been round the circuit putting his tongue down other girls' throats. The girls who give deep kissing and oral without a condom may charge a lot more than we do in my place but there's no point in being the richest working girl in the graveyard.

I've got standards. In my sauna we are old-school if you like. On Punternet you can see that the standards are changing. It's a different ball game now which is why it is hard for professional working girls in a sauna like ours to play the rules as such and still make a decent living. Why should the client come in and pay us £60 just to have a massage and hand relief or sex but can't stick his tongue down your throat and you won't give him oral without a condom. What's he going to do when he can go to a flat around the corner and get Doris to do it for £10 less including "around the world in 60 days" on a bed? Kisses, tickles, finger up her arse, tongue down her throat and everything else. Good luck to her. We call it "around the world in 60 days" when the client wants it this way, that way, your legs up there, down there. We think, here we go: "around the world in 60 days".

Chapter 20
MY NEAR DEATH
EXPERIENCE

When I had my twins I was very, very ill. So was one of the babies who was taken away from me straight away for intensive care. One of the twins was natural delivery and the other was caesarean. I ended up with a blood clot on my lung. I was transferred to another hospital. I had some dye injected into me and all sorts of tests. I was put on warfarin to thin my blood. I accidentally pulled the drip out of my arm and blood went everywhere but I pulled the panic button and they got to me in time. They kept me in hospital for two weeks and I didn't see one of the twins for four days until he came out of intensive care.

That was the time I had a near death experience. Suddenly it was all white. I was in a white corridor with a white door. Everything was white and very hazy. I know that I was running in and out of rooms trying to find my baby. I remember feeling dead and thinking I was dead. I kept running in and out of the doors and trying to get to the end of the corridor. Then there was someone or something stopping me and they were signalling me that I should go back, go back. I thought I could recognise the person at the time but I couldn't tell you now. It was just a figure repeating this gesture. Only when I woke up I realised what the gesture meant.

The nurse who was with me told me that I was very sick. She was nice and kept coming in to see me. She said "We thought we had lost you and your baby for a while. We thought we were going to have a maternal death which is very rare." Both my twins had been born before I had my near death experience. They were Max's babies but they have grown into lovely children and I love them to pieces. I am glad I was turned back from dying.

I know that there have been books about other people's near death experiences. People who have been dead on an operating table or in a car crash, say, find themselves going through a long dark tunnel towards a bright white and loving light. They can communicate with the light and they don't want to be turned away. They know that they must come back to their bodies because they aren't ready to die. They have more to do in their

155

lives.

In my experience the tunnel was a bright white corridor and the rooms leading off it were different from other people's experiences. The figure at the end of the tunnel saying "go back" is in common with my experience. Also, I know it was the right thing for me to come back. My children needed me. Being a working girl may not be the ideal way to bring up kids when the father was a villain, but I've done my best and they are in their teens now. I've tried to be as normal a mum as possible and they love me. That's what matters.

I believe in God and I did so before my near-death experience. I attended Sunday school but as an adult I've not practised any religion. My nan was very religious and as a child I went to church with her every Sunday. I go to weddings, christenings and funerals and I go to things like harvest festivals with my children. I think that God is within me. I don't pray even if I am going through a tough spot. I find it extremely hard to pray because I don't know how to pray. I do pick up the Bible now and then. I randomly open it and I randomly read it and it's funny that whatever I read at random relates to me in some way. I am a spiritual person, though. I do believe that there is a God within me, or perhaps it is a guide. I don't know what it is but I do have somebody with me.

I sometimes wonder if there is a life after dying. If it is anything like my near-death experience, then it is wonderful and nothing to be afraid of. It was so beautiful. If we are to believe that is how we go when we die and we go on to something wonderful from there, then so be it. I'm just not sure. For me, once you are gone, you're gone. What is important for me is what happens now, today. I live like that. I live for my kids. I believe that whatever there is after death must be good because the near-death experience didn't frighten me. It was warm and welcoming. It was beautiful and everything was pure and nice. But I think we have to pass the test here first before we get there and that's why I got sent back. My deeds are not done.

Apart from my near-death experience I had another experience in relation to my son. He was in Great Ormond Street and very sick and we were told to expect the worst. I sat in a little room in the hospital all night. I remember walking down a corridor in the early hours of the morning. There was a chapel there where you can go and pray. I walked in and there was nobody in there. I sat there and I fell asleep. I was so tired as I had been up for about three days. When I woke up I looked up at a figure, a big figure of Mary in the chapel. The sun was shining all through the chapel and I knew my son was alive because she told me so. Before I left that chapel I said "thank you".

I had no idea what to expect. I had been told that they had 48 hours to cultivate what was needed for my son because every organ was shutting down. They had to cultivate it to fight that disease. At Great Ormond Street they said to me "We do not pretend to you here. We do not lie to you. Your child is sick and your child is going to die if we do not find the problem". They didn't wear white coats. They were normal people.

When I left the chapel I went through the corridor and the male nurse was running down the corridor because I had special lodgings there. He was walking fast towards my room. I looked at him and I knew. I smiled and he went "Where have you been?"

"In the chapel".

He said: "Come on. We've been buzzing your room. Come on, come on. He's asking for you." They had found a drug that had kicked in when it might have been too late. But I knew from the chapel that my son was alive upstairs.

When I see commercials on TV for Great Ormond Street Hospital, I recognise that nurse and feel really happy. For me, in Great Ormond Street hospital they aren't ordinary doctors and nurses; they are gods and angels because they saved the life of my child.

I stayed in the hospital with my son for three weeks. I wasn't in a relationship at the time but I had a couple of good friends who came to see me. One was Norman, a regular client of mine who was very supportive and came to visit the hospital every day I was there. He worked in a department store and he became my rock for three weeks. Every night at about six or six-thirty I would be out at the front of Great Ormond Street smoking and there he would be turning the corner. He came because he cared for me, just to make sure I was eating and that the little one was all right. He brought teddy bears and a little lion. He was a real friend in need.

Chapter 21
HAPPY IN MY WORK?

Do I still enjoy sex?

I have sex with men every day that I am in the sauna. On a bad day it is just one client or two. On a good day it can be five. You might wonder if I still enjoy sex. The answer is that with my partner I do still enjoy it but with clients it is different. Things that clients do to me in the shop all relate to their pleasure. It's my job. It's what they are paying me.

I'm sure all working girls get clients now and then who want to give the girl a bit of real pleasure or perhaps even do so without knowing they are. There are clients who want to give the girl pleasure even before he has had his. As a rule I don't go along with it because I want to get him finished as soon as possible so that I can get on with the next one. My aim is to steer clear of that scenario and get him out of the room as quickly as I can. I just switch off. For example, if he is giving me oral and I don't want the pleasure I just switch off. I don't have to physically stop him licking me but if I switch off he could spend ten hours down there and nothing would happen. I think most of us working girls are the same.

I am an old-fashioned girl with old-fashioned values. Sometimes I feel sorry for myself that I chose the job that I do. I question myself often: if I was a nurse or worked in a supermarket would I be 100 per cent faithful to my partner? It just so happens that I am a working girl. Even so, I don't want to have sex with other men. It would make me feel guilty. I wouldn't want my partner going out and having sex with someone today either. That's how I am.

Are working girls more highly sexed than other women?

I think that some working girls go into the business not just for the money but because they really do enjoy having lots of sex. They are quite rare. I call them nymphomaniacs or maybe they are just as sexually frustrated as the clients. I've known some girls do a guy for £20. That's not about money unless they are desperate for drugs. Otherwise they must be highly sexed or oversexed and that is partly why they have gone into the game. It's

159

easy enough to go down to the pub and get fucked every night. Why go and work in a sauna if it isn't for the money! But the girls who are highly sexed and work in saunas may be very lucky and having orgasms all day long.

Mainly you have the girls who do it just for the money. You even have lesbians who work in saunas. They shag men all day long but they don't want a man in their life and they go home to a girl partner.

In my case, I was going with boys when I was in my early teens at school and I was begging to be allowed to go out with two older girls to pick up men in Earls Court but this was only for the money.

Taking working girls as a group, yes, there are a few highly sexed girls — call them nymphos if you like — who want to be satisfied sexually when they are doing a client, and there are few lesbians who only want women to satisfy them. I think that the rest of us are normally sexed and simply do it for the money. We would do other jobs if we wanted and the money was comparable. A fair number of working girls are quite well educated. They have chosen the business. They aren't victims from the bottom of the heap who have been pushed into the game. Once they are in it, they find it hard to get out and if they have got a drug addiction they are trapped. Also it is hard to get out because even if you have a qualification like I do as a state enrolled nurse, you are way out of date and would have to take lots of refresher training. You would have to explain away all the years as a working girl.

There probably aren't more highly sexed working girls than there are in any other profession or group. I know some women who work in supermarkets and who are at it every weekend. But in general I don't think working girls are highly sexed.

10 more years? No thanks

I've been in the business for 20 years and like all girls of my age I have to think about the future. The starting point is that the shop isn't making money. We don't have enough clients and I have put the shift money the girls have to pay about as high as is reasonable. The only way we can influence things is through advertising and that means cards in newsagents' windows and the internet. We put up our cards regularly and we have a website that men can access via Punternet. It is hard to know how much

160

impact they have. When men ring in and when a new client comes through the door we always ask how they heard about us. The answers are generally woolly.

If the shop was making money I could consider just being the boss, coming in once a week to pick up the cash and go to the bank. This would save me a lot of driving and stress. Also, if the shop was profitable I'd be able to sell the goodwill. I'd like to clear all my debts and have some cash in the bank to make a new start. I don't think the economy is going to pick up as far as saunas are concerned for at least a couple of years so at the moment I'm in a fix. I'm in my 40s and I know I can go on being attractive to men and a good working girl for five or even ten years if I have to. At the moment I just don't want to go on that long.

I've been living with my partner for five years and we get along OK most of the time. We have an understanding relationship which has bonded us over the years and share many secrets. Sometimes we get angry and go through days when we hardly talk to each other. Then things get better like in most relationships. He's not the father of my children but has been my rock and always has always come back to me. In all fairness I don't quite think he realised what a roller-coaster journey he was about to ride when he came into my life. He copes with my job better than I can have ever expected.

The real fathers of my children aren't much help to me. They don't support me financially in any regular way. The kids go to see them a bit but that's it.

I suppose that some working girls are lucky and find a partner they want to live with permanently. That may happen when you are in your twenties and thirties but in your forties it's much more difficult. Men don't want to marry a girl with that amount of history and by that time working girls like me have become very independent.

That's always been there in my case. My partner and I agree that we need a certain amount of independence in our lives. We may still be together in a few years from now but if we split it will be civilised and without bad feelings. I was never expecting to find a wealthy man to take care of me. That's the last thing I wanted. I just want to be able to support myself and to have enough money left over to help my kids financially as they go through school and college.

Being realistic, when you face your forties you are competing for clients against girls in their twenties. You can make up some of it with experience and keeping your prices down. In my shop we all have regulars who have been with us for five or ten years or even more, but getting new clients is the hard bit just at present and it won't get any easier. I know some girls who have face-lifts and boob jobs so that they can keep on working for a few years but that's not the way I want to go. If I am going to do that, I'm going to do it for me and not so that I can work for another five years.

I've tried getting the shifts all covered by other girls and going in to collect the money but the money wasn't coming in and I had to work myself. I don't think the girls were knocking the shop but there just wasn't enough business. I still have my regulars and I don't want to lose them to other girls so at the moment I keep working while hoping to get out. I'm aware that most of the working population on the other side of the fence may say the same thing. Some people really do love the job they do. I don't. I know that Dr Brooke Magnanti who was Belle de Jour says she really enjoyed her time as a working girl but that was only for three years.

My plan for some years has been to make enough money to do a college course. It will cost money which I don't have at the moment. I'm very good with my hands. I'm aware that if I take any kind of course I'll need to know how to use a computer. I've not done anything on that. When I was at school there weren't any computers or perhaps just one or two. I'd have to learn how to do that too.

Two things are stopping me moving on. The first is the shop which is nothing but a worry. The second is me. I'm still hiding, still having to lead a double life. I don't want to live like that anymore. My kids are getting older. I have adult conversations with them. I feel cheap. They love me so much that it's hard. I look at myself in a mirror in the shop and sometimes I feel sick. And I just think about my kids. More and more I think of them and I know that I need to get out of the business. I need to start my life again. I've toyed with the idea of going back to nursing. I loved hospital life. It would be a job that's worth while, a job I could be proud of and a bit of security as well, a job I can talk to my kids about and they can be proud of me for doing it. Even to this day they still question me. "Mum, can I come and work with you today?" It makes me feel sad.

How many years will it go on? When I had these kids and they were little I said to myself I'm not going to be doing this when they are older. I can't do this to them. I'm not going to have them asking me questions. And I'm still here. I'm still doing it.

Regrets?

Anyone can have regrets about their life. I certainly do. I'm not asking for sympathy. I made the decision to walk through the sauna door when I had been offered a job at the gym. I made the decision to quit nursing and to become an escort. I'm the one who allowed myself to support Jayden in our partnership and to stay with Max even though he beat me, abused me, had me raped and who gave me the twins. I'm the one who decided to keep the twins instead of aborting them and starting a new life without Max. I have made the decisions and I have borne the consequences. Sometimes I feel that I am being punished for what I have done and what I am.

So yes, I have regrets and yes I would lead my life differently if I had the chance. But we start from where we are now. I want to start a new life and maybe this book will be just that. If any working girl of 18 or in her twenties reads this book, I just say: do the game if you must and if that is the way you can earn most money, but stash as much as you possibly can in the bank against that day when you want to get out before it's too late. Your face and your body are your assets.

I have lost good mates to alcohol and drug abuse which still saddens me. I have been through all that and have come out the other side. But it is a constant reminder and in their case it was in vain: they paid the price. Being a working girl is a just a shell. No substance. Painful memories and hard knocks can be blotted out with alcohol, drugs, sleeping pills and painkillers. Eight out of ten working girls go and get some sort of release.

The others are normally the ones without a partner or children. They probably own their own homes and have a few quid in the bank.

I don't condemn any working girls for wanting fast money and fun too, but you will find that it comes at a price. You will certainly suffer if you become a working girl because ordinary relationships with family and friends simply don't work in the usual way. You'll find it hard to get a loyal partner. If you have kids there will soon be a day when they ask "Mum, why do you come home so late at night? " or "Mum, what do you

163

do at work"?

Lots of single mums make sacrifices for their kids and so do I. So if they find out what I was doing to bring them up — which they will never hear from me — they may think how awful. My mum was a working girl or a whore or a tart or a prostitute. They may feel ashamed of me. They may feel guilty that I had to do these things to buy them their clothes, their mobiles and the things that modern kids want. At worst they may distance themselves from me. Perhaps they will marry or settle down with a partner but never feel able to tell their partner that their mum was a working girl. If that happens I only hope that they come to see that my life as a working girl began with being all about me but then became all about them.

Working girls choose to do what we do because we see it as the easiest way to earn money. Leave aside the girls from East Europe who have been tricked and trafficked to come here by gangsters from their own countries. That is something that the law must deal with. And leave aside the girls who have to feed a drug addiction and work the streets in city centres to get their next fix. And leave aside the girls who join the business for a short period of time, for example in order to complete their university education. A spectacular case was Dr Brooke Magnanti. who first wrote a blog about being an escort, then a book and then sold the rights on the book for a television programme starring Billie Piper. She used her earnings to see herself through her PhD course in informatics. Wow!

What is left are the ordinary working girls in flats and saunas like me. We are all attractive and sometimes stunningly beautiful. Many are well educated and have trained and worked in other fields such as nursing, caring or as managers in various businesses or occupations. We have chosen to be working girls, for the money.

I trained as a state enrolled nurse and could have made that my career. I could have taken the job at the gym that I was offered. Neither of these careers would have paid me particularly well but I would have been likely to settle down and start a family with reasonable financial stability. Instead I chose to be a working girl, for the money.

To any young working girl who reads this book I just say think, think, think again. Yes, I've made awful mistakes in the men I chose as partners and you may do better, but remember there aren't many men who would want to

164

settle down with a working girl. If I had left the business years back I think that some men would have wanted me for myself but a lot of men would still not be able to take me along with my history.

If you decide that you can be a working girl for just a bit and then get out of the business, above all put money in your own bank account. Don't plan for a rainy day when your looks and your figure are on the down. Plan for a sunny day much sooner when you can take the money, buy a house or a flat, find a partner if you want one and start a new career with new training if necessary.

The terrible mistake that so many working girls make is to assume that the good times will always roll and so they save little or nothing. Learn from my mistakes. In my early days I saved and had £50k in the bank. I had a mortgage on my own house which, sadly, turned out to be far too expensive for me the moment I got pregnant. My savings melted away and anyway they were wiped out by Max's crack addiction. From then on when I had kids to support, my earnings as a working girl have kept my head above water, paid the rent on a council house and provided for my family, but that's it. I've started some bank accounts for my kids but my own bank account is always in the red and my credit cards are maxed out.

My partners have sometimes contributed to the rent and other bills but I have never counted on them to keep me or my children. Working girls learn to be tough early on and we develop an independent mindset. But our looks are our livelihood and as we get older we all want to get out of the business in some way at some time. This isn't because we hate being working girls but because it becomes harder to earn money as we get older.

We are in it for the money so when the money starts to dry up we want to get out but few of us have made plans. Going back to an ordinary job and trying to explain the great gaps in a working career is not easy. The jobs that require little training and simple skills, for example cleaning and caring, pay a low hourly rate and competition is strong from immigrants from East Europe and the Commonwealth. Walk along the corridors of any hospital in the country and you'll see what I mean.

One thing I am certain of. If I had known what life was ahead of me, what shit and traumas I've been through, I would never ever have walked through that door into the sauna. I'd be in the gym or I would have been nursing. If

165

I could turn the clock back, I would. Being a working girl took my soul into the dark side of life. Drink, drugs, some violence and a lot of misery were all paid for with my body and nearly cost my sanity.

Despite my past lifestyle which included cocaine and drinking heavily and almost wrecking my body I have managed to keep healthy and supple. As a kid, I ate, drank and breathed gymnastics. Even now I can still do the splits. I now live by the coast and often go for long walks along the beach. When nobody is near I do occasional cartwheels to prove to myself that I can still do it. The dog thinks I've gone nutty but it makes me feel younger and it helps clear my mind. Otherwise I just stay nondescript amongst the other walkers. Nobody takes any notice of me. I guess they are probably clearing out their closets too.

Chapter 22
THIS BOOK

One day I was massaging James, one of my regulars. He'd been seeing me for a few months and the chats we had in the room were more honest than most. As I worked on him I said, "You know, I could write a book about my life." This is what I've often said and heard plenty of other girls say it too. It's a pipe dream for most of us of course but we all have things to say, stories to tell about villains who have been our bosses, celebrities we have been fucked by, the highs and lows of clients requiring special services, in fact all the things you have read about in this book.

James said "That's funny. I'm a writer?" Previously he had just given one of the stock answers about his job such as "I work in an office" but this was different. "I could help you write a book about your life."

It was so sudden that I was taken aback. Was he taking the piss or hoping to get some free sessions from me? I'd always liked him and I'm pretty good at spotting men who are trying to take the piss. He wasn't one of them. "Come to my house and I'll show you" he said. "I've written books and had loads of articles in magazines and things". He didn't want to give away more than that.

A few days later I called at his house which was easy to get to between my home and the sauna. It is a semi-detached, interwar building in a good area. Its outside is smartly maintained and there is a nice little garden at the front and a larger one at the back. He lives alone so there was no worry about the time I went to see him.

My first visit was at eight one evening on my way back from a shift at the sauna. When I arrived he kissed me gently on the lips as he always does and took my coat. Then he took me into his study. It has books and files stacked on shelves round three of the walls. He showed me one particular shelf. "These are things I've written" he said. Even allowing for extra copies there were plenty of them so I could see straight off that he was telling the truth about being a writer. They had his name on the covers. Working girls seldom get to know clients' real names for obvious reasons. He was being honest with me as well as taking a risk. He clearly wanted me to trust him and here was me breaking my two golden rules: 1) never trust anyone, least of all a client; and 2) never get involved with a client outside the shop.

His study had a computer, a printer and a photocopier. He told me he worked a lot from home and went to London only when he had to. So we sat down over a coffee and talked about writing my book. He knew the ropes about publishers and agents. He told me about advances, royalties and copyrights. And he knew how to write. He'd been to university studying English. I have a GCSE in English and I don't type. His skills were just what I needed.

As we were talking he pulled open a drawer and handed me a sheet of paper. It had the title of this book at the top and underneath a table of contents with the main chapter headings. "These are the chapters and things I would want to read about if I was in a book shop and saw a book about being a working girl." There was a pause as I read them through. I looked at him and said, "Yes, I can write about all these". He was obviously pleased and I was equally pleased as I could see that I really did have a book in me waiting to be written.

He told me to begin with a chapter about my early life and my schooling. I talked a bit about the main events and I told him how I had been abused by Uncle Nick. He looked at me very sharply and said "The bastard. That was awful. Do you feel able to write about it?"

An immediate realisation came to me. The Uncle Nick episode was clear in my memory almost like an electric shock, but the pain and distress that it caused me at the time and for years afterwards were no longer there. I knew I could cope with Uncle Nick and other ugly episodes in my life. I even felt that writing about them would be the final way of getting them out of my system.

At home I found a spiral-bound exercise book and a few days later I started to write the Uncle Nick episode in long-hand. It ran to four pages and I continued with sections about my time at school and my gymnastics. I hadn't done any writing like this since my nursing exams.

When a section was finished I would tear the pages out and the next time James came to see me at the sauna I would stuff the pages into his pocket. I

168

kept them carefully hidden at home and in the sauna. We have our own locked drawers in the shop but there's not much privacy from family at home.

James got very excited by what I was writing. He just typed it out as it was and he told me that he made corrections for grammar or spelling. He said I wrote really well.

Later, to speed things up, I'd go to his house and we would go through the chapters, section by section. James asked the questions and I tape-recorded my answers. It was a dialogue with James being the interested reader and me being the working girl. The result is that everything in this book is by me. James's contribution was to give me the structure and chapter headings. He has smoothed some of the sentences but this is my book.

When you read this book I will have received a cash advance. It needs to be big enough to pay off all my credit card debts and leave enough over to put into my bank account and some for my children. I will have given a nice present to my mother who has been such a wonderful support to me throughout all the difficulties of my life, and I expect I shall have taken a short holiday on a sunny beach somewhere. Whatever is left over I want to keep carefully as my nest egg for the next part of my life.

In theory I could go on as a working girl in a sauna five or even ten years. I've still got a great figure and my face is good too. I've known working girls in their 50s still having plenty of regulars but I don't want to do that. If the sauna business picked up again, I could stop working myself and simply manage the shop, coming in to collect the cash, pay the bills and check that the girls aren't knocking the shop by not recording clients. But I am not going down that route. There are other things I want to do.

This book has been a turning point in my life financially and in other ways. Now I know that I am ready to let go of my past. I can get rid of the demons that have ruled my life, in particular the desire to have lots of money by being a working girl despite the misery and the battles inside my mind. I've always known I could do more with my life than just give pleasure to men.

There is a college course I would like to take. I might go back to being a nurse because that is emotionally fulfilling and nurses are always in

169

demand. But one thing that will satisfy me deeply for the rest of my life is the knowledge that I had it in me to write this book. I was so lucky to have met James. I did it thanks to him for providing me with continuing encouragement and a safe environment to work in. It was perfect. It enabled me to go back to the darkest corners of my mind and allowed those memories to come flooding back.

James suggested the main chapter headings and I added some more. The words are mine. If you were to meet him he'd tell you that it is my writing and my dictation. He has manuscripts and tapes to prove it. James inspired me to write the book and enabled me to get it published. I shall always love him deeply for doing that.

These are my words, this is my story and this has been my amazing life's journey. In spite of my moments of sickness and despair, I've come through against the odds. I've made it.

Printed in July 2021
by Rotomail Italia S.p.A., Vignate (MI) - Italy